# LEVI ROOTS

*Food for Friends*

My friends, I dedicate these recipes to you all – thanks for the inspiration shared. This delicious food, which has brought us together, is exciting and fresh; the vibe, chilled and mellow; the music, Roots rock reggae. So tune into the flavours and enjoy.

One love, Levi Roots

# Levi Roots' Food for Friends

First published in Great Britain in 2010 by Mitchell Beazley, an imprint of Octopus Publishing Group Limited, Endeavour House, 189 Shaftesbury Avenue, London, WC2H 8JY www.octopusbooks.co.uk

An Hachette UK Company www.hachette.co.uk

ISBN: 978 1 84533 991 3

A CIP record for this book is available from the British Library.

Set in Scala

Printed and bound in China

**Consultants** Hattie Ellis and Diana Henry
**Commissioning Editor** Becca Spry
**Senior Editor** Leanne Bryan
**Art Director** Pene Parker
**Designers** Pene Parker and Mark Kan
**Copy-editor** Lucy Bannell
**Photographer** Chris Terry
**Photographer's Assistant** Karl Bridgeman
**Home Economist** Sara Lewis
**Stylist** Wei Tang
**Proofreaders** Jo Murray and Susan McLeish
**Indexer** Helen Snaith
**Production Controller** Susan Meldrum

**Note**
This book contains some dishes made with raw or lightly cooked eggs. It is prudent for more vulnerable people such as pregnant and nursing mothers, invalids, the elderly, babies and young children to avoid uncooked or lightly cooked dishes made with eggs.

# Contents

# Introduction

This book is about making fabulocious food for your mates and family and getting the island vibe around the table. I love savouring the taste of my own cooking and get excited at the thought of other people enjoying it, but the conversation around my table is always the highlight. Tasty food brings about the best times. When my friends sit down to eat, we speak about good happenings and glad tidings. And of course there's always music, the radio's on or a CD is playing to help the vibe.

When I visit family, or they come round to my place, cooking goes on all day. My sister Jean is a regular visitor, with her husband Clint and their daughters Yvonne and Michelle. What do they eat? They like it spicy! And it warms my heart to cook with them, having them help and throw their bit in as we prepare a chicken curry and some rum punch. Laid-back and relaxed people always end up together in the kitchen. And I like that. There's never any problems apart from the pots taking too long to boil!

How did I first learn about cooking? When I was growing up in Jamaica, my grandmother taught me so much...and not just how to chop and stir. Gran was a singer in the kitchen, and the happiest ever, laughing to herself and singing at the top of her voice! She didn't sing songs exactly, she was a great 'la-la-la' lady. So she would 'la-la' all day around the cooking. You could tell she was really enjoying what she was doing.

Gran loved to cook for a lot of people, often ten or more. We had a neighbour and member of our family called Mr Butler. People would come round to his house and Gran would cook for the evening. She'd be repaid for her work by the joy of people saying the food was wonderful.

Everyone was really poor back then, so what we ate would depend on who had something to cook. If my grandfather had harvested that day – dug some yams, or got some callalloo and cabbages – we'd know we had food in abundance. And if you had too much, you'd give it away. People didn't have money to buy local food, it was just given. You'd put out what you couldn't eat and people would take it.

If it was a day when we had abundance, then my grandmother would cook round at Mr Butler's place and the visitors would bring down their work. If a family was tying tobacco leaves, they'd bring a bag of that. If someone had coffee to grind, they'd bring along the mortar and pestle. If you had some corn to shell from the husk, you'd bring four or five bagfuls. We would all share the work and talk and eat together. When the night was over, everyone went home with their work finished – all done and dusted – having had a great time eating the food while making wonderful conversation.

Those many evenings of my childhood were like witnessing your own soap opera because so much happened...and then there were the tall tales that were told! They were really outlandish stories, men talking about the most audacious events that took place. As a little boy, I was in awe. I really took in everything they said. And because they knew I was listening, they sometimes made the stories even more fantastic.

Now that I'm an adult, there are so many ways I like to get together with friends and food. As well as suppers, lunches and brunches, we may sit round a table playing a noisy game of dominoes and I'll bring out some bun and cheese (*see* page 187) and nice mangos to eat. And then Jamaicans always like to get out the barbecue and enjoy a nice piece of jerk chicken or fish. You can light up the charcoal anywhere, but the best place of all is on the beach. There are always beach parties in Jamaica, with fish-and-festival on the go, lovely white sand at your feet and a cold beer or lime wash in your hand. If you go to a beach party, you get a taste of what the real Jamaica is about. It's a free, beautiful place with real people cooking real food – no razzmatazz – but just as local people would have it.

Back home in London, Christmas is always at home with my mother and the kids. Nothing changes really, Mum wants to do everything...and we do the washing up! But as she gets older she's got to have a bit of a rest and I take over more with the food. The family comes round, we cook loads, then before the meal is eaten there's always giving thanks. The last word, before tucking in, goes to Mum or the elder at the table. It's to bless the meal and say thanks for the gathering. You have to give thanks for the little that you get or for the lot that you get.

Thinking about the way I like to cook reminds me how it goes along with music. One of my best times cooking for friends was with my band, Matic 16, before I started in the sauces business. I'd take a gas stove and my little pot on tour. Whenever we pulled up in France, Germany, Holland or anywhere, while the rest of the band was doing the soundcheck, I'd be in the dressing room, cooking up whatever local food we could grab. I always carried my seasonings, my 'Sunshine Kit' of herbs and spices, so even if we found a place where there was nothing but a sweet potato I could still nice-up the ingredients. You'd be surprised how flavoursome food can become with a bit of spicing and a chilli or two, even if you don't have much to work with.

This is how I developed my dub-it-up approach to cooking. Dub in music originated in Jamaica. You'd make a piece of music with ten musicians and instruments and the engineer would get it afterwards and start to work. He'd take the guitar out and bring it in later with a reverb put on it, or add a bit of echo, creating a fusion of sounds that became a piece of music. And you can do the same with food. I can take a typical brunch recipe or Christmas dish that is traditionally done, say, in Italy or Britain and dub it up by adding something that turns it Caribbean. If you put pimento (allspice) or Scotch Bonnet pepper into the mix, it changes the dish and adds your personality.

So get out the thyme, the fragrant heat of black pepper and the hot, fierce fruitiness of a good chilli. Bring to the stove the aromatic pimento and the exotic sweet waft of cinnamon. Seize the coriander, the zesty lime and the smooth, rich silk of some coconut milk. Mix them up for a party of flavours in your saucepan. Then pour out the rum, make one of my daiquiris (*see* page 152), call your friends and get together. This book is about how to make and eat good food with the ones you love. Blessed!

Brunch

This will seem kind of odd to British palates, but give it a go. It is quick to make and very healthy. In the Caribbean we would serve it with crackers for breakfast, but it might be more popular here with boiled rice for lunch or supper. For the photo I served them with *bammy* (rounds of pressed cassava). If you want to try them, soak cassava rounds in milk for 10 minutes, then drain well, cut into quarters and shallow-fry until golden.

# Smoked fish choka

Serves 2

320g (11½oz) smoked mackerel

4 tbsp groundnut oil

450g (1lb) tomatoes, roughly chopped

2 onions, roughly chopped

1 red pepper, deseeded and chopped into cubes, roughly 2cm (½in) square

4 garlic cloves, crushed

1 red chilli, deseeded and finely chopped

1 tbsp chopped parsley or fresh coriander (optional)

To serve

*bammy* (shallow-fried rounds of pressed cassava), cut into quarters (optional)

lime wedges (optional)

1 Flake the mackerel into large pieces and discard the skin. Set aside.

2 Pour the oil into a large frying pan and cook the tomatoes, onions, pepper, garlic and chilli over a low to medium heat, until completely soft, stirring from time to time. It will take about 20 minutes.

3 Add the fish and stir everything together to combine and heat through. Scatter with the herbs, if using. Serve with the *bammy* and lime wedges, if liked.

This is the easiest, laziest supper in the world. And it's good for you, too. You can use other soft vegetables – courgettes or mushrooms – instead of aubergine if you like. It's a complete meal in a dish, so not much washing up afterwards either!

# Lazy fish and rice

Serves 4

225g (8oz) basmati rice

vegetable oil, for the dish

1 onion, roughly chopped

1 large aubergine, cut into cubes roughly 2cm (½in) square

salt and black pepper

4 spring onions, chopped

4 garlic cloves, crushed

juice of 2 limes

leaves from 4 thyme sprigs

1 red chilli, deseeded and finely sliced

2 tbsp soy sauce

625ml (1 pint 1fl oz) hot vegetable or chicken stock

8 small mackerel fillets

lime wedges, to serve

1 Preheat the oven to 200°C/400°F/gas mark 6.

2 Put the rice in a sieve and wash it until the water runs completely clear. Brush a shallow ovenproof dish with the oil, then tip in the rice, onion and aubergine. Season well, then add all the other ingredients except the mackerel and lime wedges. Transfer to the oven and cook, uncovered, for 25 minutes.

3 Season the fish and lay the fillets on top of the ingredients in the ovenproof dish. Continue to cook for 15 minutes. When cooked, the rice will have absorbed all the stock and the fish will be cooked through. Serve with wedges of lime to squeeze over the top.

Wow! These were inspired by stuffed Mexican tortillas and the flavour combo is fabulous. If you aren't keen on smoked fish, use chorizo or any other spicy sausage instead. You can buy your rotis instead of making them (though they're very easy to make), or use Indian or Middle Eastern flatbreads and just warm them through.

# Levï's breakfast wraps

1 Preheat the oven to 190°C/375°F/gas mark 5. Put the tomatoes in a small roasting tin and drizzle over half the oil. Sprinkle over the sugar and hot pepper sauce, season, then turn the tomatoes over with your hands to cover evenly with the oil. Roast for about 40 minutes, or until the tomatoes are slightly shrunken and caramelised in places.

2 To make the rotis, sift the flour, baking powder and salt into a bowl and add 170ml (6fl oz) cold water, a little at a time. Using your hands, pull everything together to form a dough. Knead on a floured surface for about 10 minutes, until the dough is elastic. Cover and leave to rest for 10 minutes. Divide into 8 balls, roll them out very thinly and leave on a floured surface to rest for another 10 minutes.

3 Put the remaining oil in a frying pan and sauté the onion and pepper over a medium heat until the onion is soft and pale gold. Add the chilli, cumin and coriander and cook for another minute. Add the beans and cook until completely warmed through and soft. (If they fall apart a bit that's okay.) Add the lime juice and season.

4 Heat a ridged griddle or frying pan over a medium heat. Cook each roti in the dry pan on both sides until blisters appear on its surface. Be careful not to burn them. Wrap them in a cloth or transfer to an oven on a low heat to keep warm.

5 Fill each roti with some tomato, beans and fish. Put the avocado slices, yogurt and coriander on top and fold over the wrap. Cut each in half at an angle and serve.

Serves 4

8 plum tomatoes, halved

2 tbsp olive oil

2 tsp soft dark brown sugar

splash of hot pepper sauce

salt and black pepper

1 small onion, finely chopped

1 red pepper, deseeded and cubed

1 small red chilli, deseeded and finely chopped

2 tsp cumin

1 tsp coriander

400g can black beans, drained

juice of ½ lime

250g (9oz) smoked mackerel, skinned and flaked

For the rotis

225g (8oz) plain flour, plus extra to dust

1½ tsp baking powder

½ tsp salt

To serve

avocado slices

Greek yogurt

fresh coriander leaves, roughly chopped

I know the idea of energy bars is that they should be entirely good and healthy, but somehow I've got cream in my mind to pour over this... Or else you could put a bar in a school lunchbox or have it as a delicious and healthy snack-on-the-go.

# Tropical energy bar

Makes
12 pieces

1 tsp sunflower oil, for the tin

60g (2¼oz) ready-to-eat dried mango

75g (2¾oz) rolled porridge oats

25g (1oz) plain flour

50g (1¾oz) dark muscovado sugar

1 tsp ground cinnamon

really good grating of nutmeg

50g (1¾oz) shelled, unsalted pistachios

50g (1¾oz) pecans

50g (1¾oz) dates

60g (2¼oz) ready-to-eat dried apricots

2 large eggs

100g (3½oz) maple syrup

2 tbsp pumpkin seeds

1 Preheat the oven to 180°C/350°F/gas mark 4. Brush a 25 × 25cm (10 × 10in) square baking tin with the oil. Soak the dried mango in warm water for 30 minutes. Drain.

2 Put all the ingredients except the eggs, maple syrup and pumpkin seeds in a food processor. Pulse until finely chopped, but not pulverised. Put the mixture in a bowl and add the eggs, maple syrup and pumpkin seeds. Mix together, transfer to the baking tin and spread out evenly. Bake for 20–25 minutes, until light brown.

3 Allow to cool in the tin, then cut into 12 pieces. Store in an airtight container for up to 3 days.

Homemade granola is easy to make and so tasty. I like this with milk – full-fat for choice – and fresh strawberries and blueberries. It's also good with yogurt. You may even find yourself eating it just as it is – pecking away like a bird! Make sure the mango is chopped really fine as it can be a bit chewy.

# Island granola

Makes enough for 5–6 breakfasts

1 tbsp sunflower oil, plus extra for the baking sheet

150ml (5fl oz) maple syrup

1 tsp vanilla extract

225g (8oz) rolled porridge oats

100g (3½oz) pecans

pinch of salt

75g (2¾oz) dried banana chips

75g (2¾oz) dried mango, finely chopped

75g (2¾oz) fresh coconut, cut into small, thin slices

1 Preheat the oven to 140°C/275°F/gas mark 1. Oil a baking sheet.

2 Heat the oil with the maple syrup in a saucepan over a gentle heat until warm, stirring to combine. Add the vanilla extract, then stir in the other ingredients so they are well coated in the sweet mixture.

3 Spread the granola mixture over the oiled baking sheet. Bake for 20–30 minutes, stirring occasionally, until golden brown. Remove from the oven and allow to cool. Homemade granola will keep for several months if stored in an airtight container in the refrigerator.

'You have to use your inner instinct and taste to say what it is that you want.' This is the advice of Mr Porridge, famed in Kingston, Jamaica, and Brixton, London, for his wonderful concoctions. I met him in Brixton about 15 years ago but knew about him before, such is his fine reputation. Everyone in Jamaica grows up on porridge in the morning. Often it's made with cornmeal, but here I've used oats, with some of the flavourings that Mr Porridge uses to make his version so delicious.

# Mr Porridge's Jamaican porridge

Serves 4

500ml (18fl oz) milk

2 × 400ml cans coconut milk

100–200ml (3½–7fl oz) condensed milk

good grating of nutmeg

1 tsp vanilla extract

1 cinnamon stick

240g (8½oz) rolled porridge oats

large pinch of salt

½ tsp rosewater

To serve

1 banana, sliced

handful of pecans, chopped (optional)

light or dark muscovado sugar (optional)

1 Put 800ml (a scant 1½ pints) water in a large saucepan and pour in the milk, coconut milk and condensed milk. Add the nutmeg, vanilla extract and cinnamon stick. Bring to the boil, then reduce the heat, cover and simmer for 5 minutes.

2 Add the oats and salt, stir, bring back to the boil and simmer for a further 5 minutes, or until thick. Sprinkle in half the rosewater, stir and taste. Add more if you like. Remove the cinnamon stick.

3 Put the porridge in bowls. Top with the banana and, if you like, some chopped pecans and a sprinkle of muscovado sugar.

The honey in this mouth-watering shake brings out the fruitiness and goes well with the mint. And then a little bit of salt is crucial to bring out the flavour of everything. Shake it, baby!

# Tropical fruit and honey shake

Serves 4

1 ripe mango, peeled

1 banana, peeled and roughly chopped

½ papaya, peeled, deseeded and roughly chopped

450ml (16fl oz) milk

1½ tbsp runny honey

4–5 mint leaves

good grating of nutmeg

pinch of salt

To serve

crushed ice

4 mint sprigs

1 Cut the 'cheeks' off the mangos. You do this by cutting through the flesh, alongside the central stone, so that you are left with two rounded fleshy sides and a stone that still has quite a lot of fruit around it. Roughly chop the cheeks. Cut as much of the fruit from around the stone as you can.

2 Put all the ingredients in a blender and whizz thoroughly.

3 Pour the shake over crushed ice to serve. Decorate each glass with an extra sprig of mint.

When you eat pineapple, you usually cut away the skin and core and throw them away. But here's a great thrifty recipe that uses them up instead. I came across this wonderful drink at Croydon Plantation up in the hills of north Jamaica. Here they show you how many kinds of fruit grow – Jamaica is a garden of Eden. After all that learning, you're thirsty. A glass of cool, refreshing pine drink is just what you want.

# Pine drink

Serves 6

1 ripe pineapple

large piece of fresh root ginger (about 75g/2¾oz), peeled

125g (4½oz) demerara sugar

lime juice, to taste

To serve

ice cubes

6 mint sprigs (optional)

1 Cut the leaves and skin from the pineapple and reserve. Cut a thin slice from the base so it stands up on its own. Cut down the fruit to get the peel off in long strips, then make sure you get out all the little spiky 'eyes'. Cut the fruit lengthways into quarters and cut out the core and reserve. Put the fruit to one side to eat later.

2 Put the skin and core of the pineapple in a large saucepan that has a lid. Wrap the ginger in a clean dish cloth and give it a good bashing with a rolling pin; you want to really mash it up. (If you want a more fiery drink, you could whizz the ginger up in a food processor or chop it finely with a knife.) Add 1 litre (1¾ pints) water, the ginger and sugar to the pineapple pan. Cover with the lid and bring to the boil. Reduce the heat and continue cooking, still with the lid on, for 5 minutes.

3 Allow the liquid to cool, cover, then place in the refrigerator overnight, or for at least 6 hours. Strain to remove the pineapple and ginger, taste and add more sugar or a little lime juice, as desired. Serve chilled with ice cubes, either on its own or decorated with a sprig of mint.

If you decide to segment the fruit for this recipe, you can then serve it in chilled, hollowed-out citrus fruit skins (halve oranges, remove the flesh and stick the skins in the freezer). It makes a very sweet and pretty ending to a rich meal. Just serve the fruits in one of your favourite big serving bowls if that seems too tricky.

# Citrus fruits with a lime and mint syrup

Serves 6–8

150g (5½oz) caster sugar

finely grated zest and juice of 2 unwaxed limes

handful of mint leaves, plus extra to serve

1 grapefruit

2 oranges

2 blood oranges

2 pink grapefruit

1 Put 170ml (6fl oz) water in a saucepan with the sugar, lime juice and mint leaves. Bring to the boil, stirring a little to help the sugar dissolve. Boil for 10 minutes – the mixture will become syrupy – then leave to cool for the flavours to infuse for a good 40 minutes. Strain, then add the lime zest.

2 Treat each fruit as follows: cut a small slice off the top and the bottom and set on a cutting board. Using a very sharp knife, cut off the zest and pith, working from top to bottom all the way around each fruit. Now you can either cut out each segment by slicing down between the flesh and the membrane or, if this seems like too much hard work, slice the fruit into wheels. Either way, flick out any seeds you find as you go along. Put all the fruit in a broad, shallow bowl.

3 Pour the cooled syrup over the fruit and put in the refrigerator to chill. Garnish with fresh mint before serving.

I visited a great deli in Brixton Market – Wild Caper, in Market Row, off Electric Lane – where they serve a fantastic spiced sweet roots soup. The talented soup-maker told me her secret. She adds a pinch of smoked paprika for depth. I tried it in my version of the soup and it really works. Serve with a hunk of bread for a satisfying lunch!

# Roasted (Levi) Roots soup

Serves 6

2 sweet potatoes, peeled and cut into 5cm (2in) chunks

2 carrots, peeled and cut into 4cm (1½in) chunks

3 tomatoes, halved

2 red peppers, deseeded

2 red onions, quartered

3 tbsp olive oil

4cm (1½in) fresh root ginger, peeled and finely chopped

½ tsp smoked paprika, ideally Spanish, plus extra to garnish

1 tsp ground cumin

400ml can coconut milk

1 bay leaf

salt and black pepper

fresh coriander leaves, to garnish

crusty white bread, to serve

1 Preheat the oven to 200°C/400°F/gas mark 6. Toss the vegetables in the oil and roast in a roasting tin in the oven for 40 minutes, until cooked, stirring halfway through. Remove from the oven and allow to cool, then peel the skin from the peppers and tomatoes and discard. Chop the peppers.

2 Now you have two choices. I like the soup to be chunky so I chop up the roasted roots, put them in a saucepan with the remaining ingredients and 800ml (1 pint 7fl oz) water and stir everything together. Or you can put the vegetables in a blender or food processor with all the other ingredients except the bay leaf and whizz up to give a smoother soup; then you put this in a pan with 800ml (1 pint 7fl oz) water and the bay leaf and give it a good stir.

3 Season with salt. Bring to the boil, stirring, then reduce the heat to a simmer for 20 minutes to let the flavours settle down together.

4 Divide between 6 individual soup bowls, sprinkle a little smoked paprika and black pepper on top, then garnish with coriander leaves. Serve with crusty white bread.

This is a great accompaniment to meat or fish; try it with fried chicken, poached salmon or thick slices of ham. It certainly jazzes up cold meat such as Sunday roast leftovers. If you want to make it the main event, add the Parmesan.

# Pumpkin and spinach gratin

Serves 4

400g (14oz) spinach, washed and thick stalks removed

25g (1oz) block coconut cream, grated

200ml (7fl oz) double cream

salt and black pepper

25g (1oz) Parmesan cheese, grated (optional)

20g (¾oz) butter

450g (1lb) pumpkin (prepared weight), peeled, deseeded and cut into 2.5cm (1in) thick slices

4 tbsp fresh brown breadcrumbs

1 Preheat the oven to 180°C/350°F/gas mark 4. Put the spinach in a large saucepan with the water that is left clinging to the leaves after washing. Cover and set over a low heat. Cook for 4 minutes, or until wilted, turning the leaves over halfway through. Leave until cool enough to handle, then squeeze the excess water out with your hands.

2 Mix the coconut cream and double cream in a small saucepan. Heat gently over a low heat to warm through. Season and stir in the Parmesan, if you want.

3 Grease a gratin dish with half the butter. Arrange half the pumpkin in the dish, followed by the spinach, then arrange the rest of the pumpkin on top. Pour over the creamy coconut milk mixture, then sprinkle with the breadcrumbs. Dot the top of the gratin with the remaining butter.

4 Cook in the oven for 30 minutes, or until the pumpkin is tender and the gratin is a nice light, crispy brown.

In Jamaica we just love spring onions, or scallions. We often use the green parts for adding lots of flavour to dishes but here's a recipe that uses the whole vegetable. If you had a barbecue on the go – and Caribbean cooking often does – you could use that for the scallions and asparagus. Indoors, it's good to do them on a ridged griddle pan. The sauce gives a Caribbean twist to a Spanish classic and is the perfect partner to these veggies.

# Griddled spring onions and asparagus with a Romesco sauce

Serves 4

8 spring onions, trimmed

20 asparagus spears, trimmed

1 tbsp olive oil

squeeze of lime

To garnish

1 lime, quartered

handful of fresh coriander leaves, chopped (optional)

For the sauce

70g (2½oz) pecans

25g (1oz) stale white bread, crusts cut off

3 tbsp olive oil

½ garlic clove

100g (3½oz) bottled or canned piquillo peppers

½ tbsp cider vinegar

½ tsp tomato purée

small pinch of smoked paprika

1 First make the sauce: preheat the oven to 180°C/350°F/gas mark 4 and toast the pecans on a baking sheet for 10 minutes. (If you don't have stale bread, put slices of fresh bread in the oven for 3–5 minutes to dry them out.) Put the oil in a frying pan and fry the garlic and bread over a low heat, until browned. Put all the sauce ingredients in a blender or food processor with 2–3 tbsp water. Whizz to a thick consistency, adding a little more water if necessary.

2 Heat a ridged griddle pan over a high heat for 5 minutes. Toss the spring onions and asparagus in the olive oil. Cook on the griddle, in batches, turning halfway through. Allow the vegetables to cool then season with the squeeze of lime. Serve with the sauce, at room temperature, and garnish with griddled lime quarters, and fresh coriander leaves, if you like.

When I flew to Britain from Jamaica as a boy aged 11 my first taste of foreign food was baked beans on the plane. Agghhhh! I just wasn't used to processed food after all the fresh produce I ate on my grandparents' farm. But here's a dubbed-up, homemade version of the dish that is so easy to prepare and fills the kitchen with warmth and good aromas. It's great served on toast or with sausages or ham. Remember, you'll have to soak the beans the night before cooking.

# Levi's baked beans

Serves 10,
on toast

500g (1lb 2oz) dried haricot beans

2 garlic cloves, roughly chopped

4 tbsp tomato purée

3 tbsp maple syrup

3 tbsp soft light brown sugar

3 tbsp cider vinegar

1 large onion, halved and stuck with 2 cloves

2 tsp salt

3 bay leaves

1 tsp ground allspice

fresh coriander leaves, to garnish

1 Cover the beans with water and leave to soak, covered, overnight. The next day, drain the beans, rinse and tip into a large casserole dish that has a lid. Add enough water to cover by a couple of fingers' depth and bring to the boil, skimming off any impurities that rise to the surface.

2 Boil the beans hard for 10 minutes, then reduce the heat. Simmer, covered, for between 30 minutes and 1 hour, or until tender, checking occasionally that the water hasn't boiled away and adding more to cover if necessary. The time taken can vary greatly depending on the age and condition of the beans.

3 Preheat the oven to 140°C/275°F/gas mark 1. Stir all the remaining ingredients except the coriander leaves into the pan with the beans and add enough fresh water to cover. Replace the lid and bake for 2 hours. Stir the beans, add more water if necessary, cover and return to the oven for 1 hour. Adjust the seasoning to taste and serve garnished with fresh coriander leaves. These beans also keep well in the refrigerator for a couple of days.

This is a wonderfully sweet and filling salad, with the silky avocado and griddled sweet potato slices bathed in a dubbed-up dressing.

# Warm salad of avocado, roast pepper and sweet potato

Serves 4

2 red peppers, deseeded and quartered

1½ tbsp olive oil, plus extra for the sweet potatoes

salt and black pepper

2 sweet potatoes, peeled

2 ripe avocados

squeeze of lemon juice

225g (8oz) rocket, baby spinach, watercress or lambs' lettuce

For the dressing

1 tbsp sherry vinegar

smidgen of Dijon mustard

½ small red chilli, deseeded and finely sliced

½ tsp caster sugar

4 tbsp extra-virgin olive oil

splash of rum (optional)

1 Preheat the oven to 190°C/375°F/gas mark 5. Put the peppers in a roasting tin, drizzle with the oil, season and roast for about 30 minutes, or until soft. At the same time, wrap the sweet potatoes in foil and place them in the oven. Roast until only just tender (you are going to cook them more so you don't want them to be too soft). Place the peppers in a sealed plastic bag to cool.

2 Make the dressing by whisking all the ingredients together. Add salt and pepper to taste.

3 Halve the avocados, remove the stones and cut the flesh into slices lengthways, with the skin still attached. Carefully peel the skin from each slice. Squeeze a little lemon juice over the avocado pieces to prevent them from discolouring, then season.

4 Remove the peppers from the plastic bag, peel and discard the skins, then cut the flesh into strips. Slice the potatoes into rounds about the thickness of your little finger. Brush these with oil and season all over. Heat a ridged griddle pan and cook the potatoes on both sides so they take on lovely scorch marks.

5 Gently toss the potatoes, pepper strips, avocado slices and leaves together with the dressing. Serve immediately.

I love the sweet heat of chilli against the clean taste of healthy spinach and squash. Peanuts (from a packet is fine) finish off the whole salad beautifully. Try this with spicy roast chicken or pork.

# Roast squash, chilli and spinach salad with peanut and ginger dressing

Serves 6
as a side dish

1kg (2lb 4oz) butternut squash, halved, deseeded and cut into 1cm (½in) wide slices

3 tbsp olive oil

salt and black pepper

1 tsp caster sugar

2 red chillies, deseeded and cut into slivers

150g (5½oz) baby spinach leaves

For the dressing

1¾ tsp white wine vinegar

smidgen of Dijon mustard

1 piece of preserved stem ginger in syrup, finely chopped, plus 1 tsp syrup

5 tbsp groundnut oil

25g (1oz) roasted peanuts, roughly chopped

1 Preheat the oven to 200°C/400°F/gas mark 6.

2 Place the squash on a baking sheet. Drizzle with the oil, season, then sprinkle with the sugar. Turn over with your hands, making sure the squash gets well coated with the oil. Roast for 25 minutes, scattering over the chilli for the last 10 minutes. Leave to cool a little.

3 To make the dressing, put the vinegar, mustard, ginger and syrup in a cup and season. Whisk in the oil with a fork. Adjust the seasoning, to taste. Stir in the peanuts.

4 Gently toss the spinach and squash together with the dressing. Serve immediately.

Tilapia is a firm, meaty farmed fish that's easy to cook and relatively cheap. These fish cakes are good for a brunch dish, or serve them with a salad for a light lunch or supper. They're also great with my Sticky Red Cabbage (*see* page 120).

# Golden tilapia fishcakes

Serves 4

500g (1lb 2oz) sweet potatoes, cut into small chunks

4 skinned tilapia fillets (about 450g/1lb in total)

200ml (7fl oz) milk or water

zest of 1 lime, finely grated

good grating of nutmeg

2 spring onions, green part only, finely chopped

1 hot red chilli (ideally Scotch Bonnet), deseeded and finely chopped

salt and black pepper

1–2 tbsp olive oil

1 lime, quartered, to serve (or use the grated one)

For the coating

60g (2¼oz) plain flour

100g (3½oz) breadcrumbs

1 Put the sweet potatoes in a saucepan of water, bring to the boil, then reduce the heat and simmer for 5 minutes, or until cooked. Drain well. Meanwhile, put the tilapia fillets in a saucepan and just cover with the milk or water. Bring to the boil, cover, turn off the heat and leave to sit for 5 minutes to gently cook the fish.

2 Mash the sweet potato in a mixing bowl. Add the lime zest, nutmeg, spring onions and chilli. Take the fish out of the pan, pat it dry and cut it into small pieces. Mix into the sweet potato mash and season.

3 To coat the fishcakes, spread out the flour on one small plate and the breadcrumbs on another. Divide the fishcake mixture into 8 equal-sized balls and shape each into a fishcake about 2.5cm (1in) thick. Coat each fishcake first in flour, then in breadcrumbs.

4 Heat the oil in a frying pan over a medium heat and cook the fishcakes, in batches, on both sides, until they are golden brown and hot all the way through (about 8 minutes). Serve with lime wedges.

You will need good fresh prawns for this recipe, as their stock is important for the flavour. I sometimes add cubed and cooked sweet potato or waxy potato, or even squash, to make the dish go further. This is great served with plain boiled rice.

# Creole prawns

Serves 4–5

500g (1lb 2oz) raw prawns, shell on

150ml (5fl oz) dry white wine

1 onion, half roughly chopped, half finely chopped

few celery leaves

3 tbsp olive oil

4 garlic cloves, roughly chopped

1 green pepper, deseeded and cubed

1 red pepper, deseeded and cubed

½ tbsp hot paprika

1 tsp ground cumin

395g can tomatoes in thick juice

1 tsp soft light brown sugar (or to taste)

salt and black pepper

2 tbsp chopped fresh coriander leaves, to garnish

lime wedges, to serve

1 Pull the heads and shells off the prawns and remove the little legs. With a sharp knife, make a shallow cut down the back of each prawn and, with your fingers or a cocktail stick, remove and discard the black vein. Put the shells in a saucepan with the wine, roughly chopped onion and celery leaves. Simmer for 30 minutes, then strain into a bowl, reserving the stock.

2 Pour the oil into a saucepan and sauté the finely chopped onion, garlic and peppers over a medium heat, until soft. Stir in the paprika and cumin and cook for 1 minute, then add the tomatoes and juice, sugar and the prawn shell stock. Season to taste.

3 Simmer the mixture for about 20–30 minutes, until it becomes thick, then add the prawns and cook gently for 4 more minutes to heat everything through. Garnish with fresh coriander leaves and serve with lime wedges.

This gives a dub-it-up Caribbean twist to the French classic *moules marinières*. Fabulocious!

# Coconut chilli mussels

Serves 4
as a light starter
or lunch

2kg (4lb 8oz) mussels

400ml can coconut milk

2 red onions, thickly sliced

4 spring onions, green parts only, thickly sliced

2 garlic cloves, finely chopped

1 hot red chilli (ideally Scotch Bonnet), seeds left in or removed, depending on how hot you like it, finely chopped

finely grated zest and juice of 1 unwaxed lime

2 tbsp chopped fresh coriander leaves, to garnish (optional)

crusty bread, to serve (optional)

1 Prepare the mussels by scrubbing them under running water and pulling away the 'beard' (the threads coming out of the side of the shell). Discard any that are cracked, or that are open and do not close when tapped on the side of the sink.

2 Pour the coconut milk into a large casserole that has a lid, and add the red onions, spring onions, garlic, chilli, lime zest and juice. Simmer over a gentle heat for 15 minutes.

3 Add the mussels to the casserole, put on the lid and allow to steam over a low heat for 5–8 minutes, giving them a shake or a stir a few times. Check the shells are open and the shellfish are cooked.

4 Spoon the mussels into 4 large bowls, discarding any that haven't opened. Spoon over the liquor. Sprinkle with the fresh coriander leaves and serve with crusty bread, if you like.

Picnic

This is a favourite in the southern states of America, but it also sits well in Caribbean meals as it uses ingredients that are loved there. If you have trouble getting buttermilk, then use soured cream mixed with milk, adding enough milk to a small tub of cream to bring it up to 170ml (6fl oz). This bread is fabulous with spicy roast chicken and greens, or with breakfast fish dishes such as my Smoked Fish Choka (*see* page 16).

# Crispy corn bread

Serves 6

knob of lard, for the tin

1 tbsp groundnut oil

4 spring onions, green parts only, finely chopped

1 small red chilli, deseeded and finely sliced

125g (4½oz) canned sweetcorn, drained

150g (5½oz) cornmeal or fine polenta

15g (½oz) plain flour

¾ tbsp baking powder

1 tsp baking soda

good pinch of salt

1 tbsp caster sugar

1 egg, beaten

170ml (6fl oz) buttermilk

15g (½oz) butter, melted

1 Preheat the oven to 210°C/410°F/gas mark 6½. Grease a round, 5cm (2in) deep, 20cm (8in) wide cake tin with the lard and put it in the oven to get very hot. Heat the oil in a frying pan over a medium heat and sauté the spring onions, chilli and sweetcorn for about a minute to soften the onions and chilli. Remove from the heat.

2 Sift all the dry ingredients together into a bowl. Mix the egg with the buttermilk in a jug. Make a hollow in the middle of the dry ingredients and gradually pour the buttermilk mixture into this, bringing in the dry ingredients as you do so with a fork. Add the melted butter and the spring onion mixture.

3 Carefully take the cake tin out of the oven and pour the corn batter into it – it should sizzle. Return the tin to the oven and bake the bread for 15–20 minutes, until it is golden and the edges are starting to come away from the sides of the tin. Turn out on to a wire rack to cool. Cut into wedges to serve.

This is a warm, sweet and savoury salad with a bit of a kick. It's very good for you, too. It's great for vegetarians, but if you want to beef it up then chunks of sautéed bacon or very spicy sausage (try chorizo) are fabulous in it. Great for a picnic!

# Corn bread, tomato and avocado salad

Serves 8 as
a side dish,
6 as a starter

1 quantity Crispy Corn Bread
(*see* page 48)

800g (1lb 12oz) tomatoes, halved
or quartered, depending on size

2 avocados, sliced

300g (10½oz) baby spinach leaves

For the dressing

3 tbsp balsamic vinegar

7 tbsp olive oil

pinch of caster sugar

1 long red chilli, deseeded
and finely sliced

salt and black pepper

1 Preheat the oven to 190°C/375°F/gas mark 5. To make the dressing just mix all the ingredients together, whisking with a fork, and season to taste.

2 Break the corn bread into chunks and put it on to a baking sheet. Bake in the oven for about 8 minutes, or until lightly toasted.

3 Gently toss all the salad ingredients together in a broad shallow bowl with the dressing while the cornbread is still hot. Serve in individual salad bowls. For a picnic, carry the dressing in a separate container and dress the salad just before serving.

I love the sunny look of this tart and the combination of the sweet potato and onion with the salty feta and hot chilli. It's great for a picnic, or you could serve it as a starter with salad, or even as a light main course, if you added some French beans.

# Sweet potato, red onion and feta sunshine tart

Serves 4–5

225g (8oz) sheet ready-made shortcrust pastry

1 tbsp olive oil

2 red onions, finely chopped

leaves from a large thyme sprig, plus extra to garnish

200g (7oz) sweet potato, cut into 5mm (¼in) slices

100g (3½oz) feta, cut into 2cm (¾in) dice

1 hot red chilli (ideally Scotch Bonnet), deseeded and finely sliced

3 eggs

6 tbsp crème fraîche (about 90ml/3¼fl oz)

black pepper

1 Preheat the oven to 200°C/400°F/gas mark 6. Roll the pastry sheet out a little thinner and transfer it to a 25cm (10in) diameter non-stick metal tart case. Trim the pastry around the edges. Put a sheet of greaseproof paper on top of the pastry and fill with baking beans. Bake for 10 minutes, remove the parchment and baking beans and return to the oven for another 3 minutes or so, to dry out the bottom of the pastry. Remove from the oven and reduce the temperature to 180°C/350°F/gas mark 4. Put a baking sheet in the oven to warm.

2 Meanwhile, heat the oil in a frying pan and gently fry the onions with the thyme, until soft (about 15 minutes). Spread the onions over the base of the cooled pastry case. Arrange the sweet potato, feta and chilli over the top. Crack the eggs into a bowl and mix well with the crème fraîche. Spoon this over the contents of the tart, spreading it evenly. Garnish with extra thyme leaves and season well with black pepper (the tart won't need salt because of the salty feta).

3 Transfer the tart to the hot baking sheet in the oven and cook for 25–30 minutes, until set firm and golden. Check during this time that the edges of the pastry aren't scorching; if they are, cover the tart with foil. Serve hot, warm or cold.

Although it is a celebrated English summertime salad and sandwich filling, Coronation chicken is often done very badly. This super-spicy version with fresh fruit and my Mango and Ginger Chutney (*see* page 126) is the business. And it's great for a summer picnic with a friend.

# Super regal coronation chicken

Serves 4

1 tsp ground allspice

1½ tsp curry powder

250g (9oz) mayonnaise

550g (1lb 4oz) cold roast chicken breast, cut into strips or chunks

6 tbsp plain Greek yogurt

6 tbsp Mango and Ginger Chutney (*see* page 126)

1 red chilli, deseeded and finely sliced

generous squeeze of lime

salt and black pepper

To serve

mango slices

watercress leaves

toasted flaked almonds

1 Stir the spices into the mayonnaise, then gently mix all the ingredients together. Adjust the seasoning and amount of chilli to taste.

2 Serve the chicken with slices of mango and watercress leaves, with the toasted almonds sprinkled on top.

This is a more moist, thinner flapjack than some, and is very moreish. Dried bananas are a tropical treat – they're good on their own, but also delicious in this dish.

# Banana and honey flapjacks

Makes 12 pieces

175g (6oz) unsalted butter, plus extra for the tin

25g (1oz) light muscovado sugar

1 tbsp honey

1½ tbsp golden syrup

1 large ripe banana

300g (10½oz) rolled porridge oats

75g (2¾oz) dried banana chips

1 Preheat the oven to 180°C/350°F/gas mark 4. Generously butter a 21 × 22cm (8¼ × 8½in) shallow tin. Melt the rest of the butter in a saucepan. Add the sugar, honey and syrup and heat gently, stirring occasionally, until everything is melted and mixed. Remove the pan from the heat and leave to cool slightly.

2 Mash the banana in a mixing bowl, then stir in the buttery syrup and the oats. Spread half the mixture in the prepared tin and sprinkle with the banana chips. Spread the rest of the oat mixture on top and press down to compact. (You need to make sure the banana chips are wedged down within the mixture and not on top or they will burn.)

3 Bake the mixture in the centre of the oven for 25–30 minutes, or until golden brown. Remove from the oven and, using a knife, mark immediately into 12 even-sized pieces. As the flapjack cools it will hold together. Allow to cool completely in the tin, then slice into 12 pieces. Store in an airtight container and eat within a few days.

Barbecue
and Grill

The oiliness of mackerel is just great with the subtle taste of avocado – be sure to have some of both in each mouthful. You can either barbecue or grill the fish for this dish. Plain rice and a spinach salad or sweet roasted peppers are lovely on the side.

# Spiced mackerel with avocado mash

Serves 4

4 mackerel, gutted and degilled (head and tail left intact)

lemon or lime wedges, to serve

For the marinade

2 tsp coriander seeds

1 tsp ground mixed spice

2 tsp ground allspice

2 tsp black peppercorns

2.5cm (1in) fresh root ginger, peeled and finely chopped

1 tsp cumin seeds

juice of 2 limes

1 tbsp olive oil, plus extra for the foil

For the mash

2 avocados

2 tsp white wine vinegar

juice of 1 lime

1 garlic clove, crushed

good handful of mint leaves, roughly chopped

salt and black pepper

1 Put everything for the marinade (except the oil) in a large mortar. Grind with a pestle, then add the oil and mix to a paste. Wash the mackerel inside and outside and pat dry with kitchen paper, then spread the marinade all over the fish, both inside and out. Put in a non-reactive dish, cover with clingfilm and refrigerate for 15–30 minutes, until you want to cook them. Don't leave it longer than an hour or the lime juice will 'cook' the fish.

2 You need to make the avocado mash at the last minute, otherwise it will discolour. Halve the avocados, remove the stones and mash the flesh in a bowl with all the other ingredients. Adjust the seasoning to taste.

3 If you are going to barbecue the fish, place them in individual foil parcels, drizzling a little more oil over them to ensure that they don't stick. Barbecue the parcels over medium-hot coals for about 5 minutes, turning halfway through, until done.

4 If you are cooking this under a grill, heat the grill to its highest setting, place the fish on oiled foil on a grill rack or baking sheet and grill for 5 minutes. Then turn the grill off, close the oven door and leave for 4 minutes more – the residual heat will finish the cooking. You don't need to go to the bother of turning the fish over.

5 Serve the mackerel immediately with wedges of lemon or lime and accompanied by the avocado mash.

This is such a pretty dish, with the pink of the prawns in contrast to the white of the coconut. Make it with fresh grated coconut if you have the time, otherwise desiccated is fine. You can enjoy this as a simple yet exotic starter or make it more of a main meal by serving with rice and a salsa. You will need 10 wooden skewers.

# Coconut king prawns

Serves 5 as a starter
(makes about 10 skewers)

300g (10½oz) peeled raw king prawns, tails left on

finely grated zest and juice of 1 lime

¼ hot red chilli (ideally Scotch Bonnet), deseeded and finely chopped

50g (1¾oz) freshly grated coconut or unsweetened desiccated coconut

black pepper

lime wedges, to serve (optional)

1 Put the prawns in a shallow non-reactive dish and mix with the lime zest and juice and the chilli. Cover and leave to marinate in the refrigerator for 1 hour. Meanwhile, soak the wooden skewers in cold water for at least 30 minutes, to help prevent them from burning, and line a baking sheet with foil.

2 Heat the grill to its highest setting. Spread the coconut on a plate and mix it with plenty of black pepper. Take the prawns out of the marinade and thread them on to the skewers (about 4 prawns per skewer). Coat the prawns in coconut on one side. Put them, coconut-side up, on the baking sheet and cook under the grill for 1½–2 minutes, until the coconut is starting to brown in parts.

3 Coat the other side of the prawn skewers in the coconut mixture and grill on this side, again until the coconut is starting to brown slightly. The prawns will be pink when they're cooked. Serve with lime wedges, if liked.

I can't resist the sweet, smoky taste of coconut cooked on the barbecue. This recipe is a winner. Just make sure you move the chicken further away from the coals after it has coloured on each side, so it cooks through but doesn't burn. This can also be grilled.

# Coconut and thyme barbecue chicken

Serves 6

12 bone-in chicken thighs, skin left on

For the marinade

2 × 400g cans coconut cream

2 tbsp soft light brown sugar

finely grated zest and juice of 2 limes

2 tsp white wine vinegar

6 garlic cloves, crushed

leaves from 8 thyme sprigs, chopped

2 red chillies, deseeded and finely shredded

1 Put all the ingredients for the marinade, except the chillies, in a blender or food processor and whizz. Taste to check it has a good balance of sweetness and sourness. Adjust by adding a little more sugar or vinegar, if necessary. Stir in the chilli.

2 Pierce the chicken on the flesh side (not the skin side) with a sharp knife. Put the pieces in a dish and pour the marinade over the top. Turn the chicken to make sure all the pieces are well coated. Cover with clingfilm and refrigerate for at least 1 hour and up to 24 hours. Turn the chicken pieces over every so often.

3 Lift the chicken out of the marinade. Either heat a barbecue until the flames have died down to medium-hot grey ash, or heat a grill to a medium-hot setting. If using a barbecue, cook the chicken pieces for about 3 minutes on each side, until coloured, then move further away from the coals and continue to cook for about 15 minutes, until the chicken is cooked through (pierce the thickest piece of chicken with a skewer – if the juices run clear, it is done; if not, give it another 5 minutes, then test again).

4 If you are cooking this under a grill, line a baking sheet with foil and put the chicken on top, underside up. Cook under the medium-hot grill, until golden (around 3–4 minutes). Turn over, spoon on some more of the marinade, and continue to grill until this side, too, is golden (another 3–4 minutes). Reduce the grill's heat to low and cook for 15 minutes, or until the chicken is completely cooked through, with no trace of pink juices (check as above).

This simple, tasty dish is great for a barbecue, or for supper if you are cooking and eating indoors. Marinate the meat for a few hours if you can, to let it really juice up and drink in the flavours. You will need 12 wooden skewers. Serve with plain rice, or my Red, Green and Gold Coconut Rice (*see* page 131).

# Grilled lime and honey chicken skewers

Serves 4

2 tbsp soy sauce

juice of 4 limes

2 tbsp honey

½ tbsp sunflower oil

black pepper

8 boneless, skinless chicken thighs

1 Marinate the chicken at least a couple of hours before you want to eat – and ideally overnight. Mix together the soy sauce, lime juice, honey and oil in a non-reactive dish. Season well with plenty of black pepper. If the honey is thick, it'll soon dissolve, just stir it a couple of times. Cut each chicken thigh into 5 pieces. Mix well with the marinade, cover with clingfilm and put in the refrigerator.

2 Soak the wooden skewers in cold water for at least 30 minutes before cooking, to help prevent them from burning. Thread 3–4 pieces of meat on to each skewer, concertina style.

3 Either heat a barbecue until the flames have died down to hot grey ash, or heat a grill to its highest setting. Barbecue the skewers for about 10 minutes or so, turning and basting a couple of times with the remaining marinade, until the outside of the chicken is golden brown and the inside cooked through (pierce the thickest piece of chicken with a skewer – if the juices run clear, it is done; if not, give it another 5 minutes, then test again).

4 If you are cooking this under a grill, line a baking sheet with foil and put the chicken skewers on top. Pour over all the marinade. Cook under the hot grill for 5 minutes, turn over and baste. Cook for 5 minutes more, turn again and cook for a final minute or so until the chicken is cooked through (check as above). Spoon over the sticky sauce, which will have reduced down (some will have burnt, so just leave that), and serve.

This Cuban dish can be roasted in the oven as well as cooked on a barbecue. If you want to, use bone-in chicken thighs and cook at 190°C/375°F/gas mark 5 for 35 minutes. Or marinate a whole 1.6kg (3½lb) chicken and roast it at the same temperature for 1½ hours, although you may have to cover the bird with foil to stop it becoming too dark. This is great enjoyed with an ice-cold beer!

# Barbecue chicken with mojo

Serves 6

12 boneless chicken thighs

For the marinade

3 tsp cumin seeds

6 garlic cloves

2 red chillies, deseeded

salt, to taste

4 tbsp olive oil

5 tbsp freshly squeezed orange juice

5 tbsp lime juice

To serve

chargrilled sweetcorn cobs, halved

chargrilled orange and lime wedges

1 First make the marinade. Place a heavy, medium-sized frying pan over a medium-high heat and toast the cumin seeds for about 2 minutes, until they release their spicy smell (they will become slightly darker in colour).

2 Put the cumin in the bowl of a small food processor and add the garlic and chilli with a little salt. Grind to a coarse paste, then scrape into a small bowl. Heat the oil in the same frying pan until very hot and pour it over the paste, stirring to blend. Leave to stand for about 15 minutes, then whisk the orange and lime juices into the paste and set aside to cool completely.

3 Pierce the pieces of chicken on the flesh side (not the skin side) with a sharp knife. Put them in a non-reactive dish in a single layer and pour over the marinade. Turn the chicken to make sure all the pieces are well coated. Cover with clingfilm and refrigerate for at least 1 hour and up to 5 hours.

4 Heat a barbecue until the flames have died down to medium-hot grey ash. Lift the chicken out of the marinade and cook on the barbecue, basting every so often with the leftover marinade. Once the pieces have coloured on each side, which will take about 2 minutes, move the chicken further away from the coals and continue to cook for 8–10 minutes, until cooked all the way through (pierce the thickest piece of chicken with a skewer – if the juices run clear, it is done; if not, give it another 5 minutes, then test again).

5 Serve with chargrilled sweetcorn cobs and chargrilled orange and lime wedges.

This dish has a mixture of refreshing flavours that are typical of the Caribbean. It's a whole new take on the lamb chop! If you can plan ahead, it is worthwhile marinating the chops for a long time – 24 hours is good and 48 is even better – to really get the flavours right into the meat. But it is also tasty after just a couple of hours if you forget. You will need 16 small wooden skewers.

# Lime and thyme lamb chops

Serves 4

| | |
|---|---|
| large bunch of thyme | 2.5cm (1in) fresh root ginger, peeled |
| 4 tbsp lime juice | 1 tbsp olive oil |
| 1 tbsp finely grated lime zest | ½ tsp salt |
| 4 tbsp syrup from a jar of preserved stem ginger | 1 hot red chilli (ideally Scotch Bonnet) |
| | 8 loin lamb chops |

1 Soak the wooden skewers in cold water for at least 30 minutes before cooking, to help prevent them from burning.

2 Remove any really woody, thick parts of the thyme and put the rest in the bowl of a small food processor with all the other ingredients except the lamb. If you like, take the seeds out of the chilli, or leave them in for a hotter dish. Whizz up to get a marinade; it doesn't have to be completely smooth.

3 Skewer each of the chops with 2 wooden skewers to stop them from coming apart during cooking, place in a shallow, non-reactive dish and cover with the marinade. Cover the dish with clingfilm, refrigerate and leave to marinate for up to 48 hours, turning the chops over a couple of times. Take the dish out of the refrigerator 30 minutes before cooking to take the chill off the meat.

4 Either heat a barbecue until the flames have died down to medium-hot grey ash, or heat a grill to a medium setting. Cook the chops, turning a couple of times, until cooked through (they should take 2–3 minutes on each side for rare and 3–4 minutes on each side for well done). Alternatively, fry the chops until cooked through and then pour the rest of the marinade into the frying pan to make a gravy, stirring up the lovely flavours from the bottom of the pan.

It is so hard to think of new and interesting things to do with pork chops, so this is a recipe for all those cooks in need of inspiration for cooking for friends. These are lovely with my Red, Green and Gold Coconut Rice (*see* page 131).

# Calypso pork chops

Serves 6

6 pork chops (about 300g/10½oz each)

3 tbsp sunflower oil

salt and black pepper

For the marinade

10 tbsp dark soft brown sugar

juice of 3 limes

2 red chillies, deseeded and roughly chopped

2 garlic cloves, crushed

1 tsp ground ginger

4 tbsp rum

splash of angostura bitters (optional)

To serve

lime wedges, for squeezing

fresh coriander leaves (optional)

1 Mix all the marinade ingredients together in a non-reactive bowl. Place the chops in the marinade, turn so all sides are coated, cover with clingfilm and leave to marinate in the refrigerator for several hours, or up to 24 hours. Turn the chops over every so often.

2 Heat 2 frying pans until they are really hot and take the chops out of the marinade, scraping any that is clinging to them back into the bowl. Brush the chops all over with the oil, then season. Cook them in the frying pans over a high heat for about 3 minutes, or until you get a good colour, then turn over and repeat on the other side.

3 Reduce the heat to low and continue to cook the chops until cooked through – this takes at least 10 minutes. There should be no pink juices left when you pierce the meat. Towards the end of the cooking time, add the marinade and let it glaze the pork chops and bubble away in the pan. Squeeze on some lime and scatter with fresh coriander, if you like, before serving.

This sticky jerk marinade is deliciously sweet: the pineapple juice is really noticeable in the end taste and the jerk flavourings buzz your tastebuds!

# Sticky jerk spare ribs

Serves 4

16 spare ribs

1 onion, quartered

1 celery stick, cut into 4 pieces

10 allspice berries

For the marinade

2 tbsp vegetable oil

2 tbsp soft dark brown sugar

4 tbsp mango chutney

200ml (7fl oz) pineapple juice

1 tsp salt

½–1 tsp cayenne pepper, to taste

½ tsp ground cinnamon

¾ tbsp ground ginger

1 Place the spare ribs, onion, celery and allspice berries in a large saucepan. Cover with water, bring to the boil and simmer for 1 hour.

2 Meanwhile, put all the marinade ingredients in a saucepan and place over a medium heat. Give the mixture a good stir, bring to the boil, then reduce the heat and simmer very gently for 20 minutes, stirring occasionally, to get a sticky sauce.

3 Drain the spare ribs and discard the onion, celery and allspice berries. Coat the ribs with the sticky sauce and let cool slightly, then cover with clingfilm and leave to marinate in the refrigerator for at least 4 hours, or, ideally, overnight. Turn the chops over every so often. Take the ribs out of the refrigerator 30 minutes before you want to cook them.

4 Either heat a barbecue until the flames have died down to hot grey ash, or heat a grill to its highest setting. If using a barbecue, cook the ribs, turning occasionally, until the outside is browned and the inside cooked through. If you are cooking this under a grill, line a baking sheet with foil and put the ribs on top, making sure they are evenly coated with sauce. Grill until the meat is charred on the outside and cooked through, turning once or twice.

This is a show-stopper of a burger, both in looks and taste. The 'sunshine' comes from the hot Jamaican flavourings and the melted cheese. Adapt the jerk seasoning as you like, according to your tastes, making it as hot as you can handle.

# Sunshine burger

Serves 4

700g (1lb 9oz) lean minced beef

2 tbsp chopped fresh coriander leaves

2 spring onions, green parts only, very finely chopped

1 tbsp sunflower oil

4 large burger buns

4 slices of Red Leicester cheese

4 thin slices of red onion

4 slices of beef tomato

4 round slices of green pepper

For the jerk seasoning

1–2 tsp cayenne pepper, to taste

leaves from 4 thyme sprigs

½ tsp ground allspice

1 tsp black pepper

½–1 tsp salt

To serve

4 tbsp Sunshine Kit Cooking Sauce (*see* page 123)

4 fresh coriander leaves (optional)

1 Put the mince in a bowl and use your hands to mix it together well with the chopped coriander leaves and spring onions. In a small bowl, combine all the ingredients for the jerk seasoning, then add this to the meat, mixing well. Divide the mixture into 4 and shape each piece into a large burger, about 2cm (¾in) thick.

2 Heat the oil in a large frying pan and cook the burgers over a medium heat, turning a couple of times, for about 8 minutes, until cooked through. Meanwhile, either heat a barbecue until the flames have died down to hot grey ash, or heat a grill to its highest setting.

3 Halve the burger buns and lightly toast on the barbecue or on a baking sheet under the grill. Top the bun bases with a burger, a slice of cheese, then slices of onion, tomato and pepper. Barbecue or grill until the cheese melts and bubbles. Top with spoonfuls of my Sunshine Kit Cooking Sauce, garnish with the fresh coriander leaves, if liked, then cover with the bun tops – and enjoy!

This is the simplest barbecue pudding there is. Sling the bananas on the barbie and let the heat do the work. If you don't like passion fruit (or think they're a bit expensive), then slit the bananas down their tummies and spoon on sweetened cream (maybe with a bit of rum added) and grated chocolate. Hot banana and cold cream is fabulocious.

# Barbecue bananas with passion fruit cream

Serves 8

8 bananas

300ml (½ pint) whipping cream

4 tbsp lemon or orange curd

8 passion fruit

icing sugar, to taste, plus extra to dust

1 Set the bananas – in their skins – on the bars of your barbecue, close to medium-hot coals. Leave to cook until the skins are black and the flesh inside feels soft when you pierce it with a skewer.

2 Meanwhile, whip the cream until it holds its shape, then stir in the curd. Halve the passion fruit and scoop out the pulp and seeds with a teaspoon. Strain this, then remove and discard half the seeds. Return the rest to the juice and pulp. Mix half the passion fruit into the cream. Taste to see if you want to add any icing sugar (passion fruit can be very tart so even with the curd you may want to add some more sweetness).

3 When the bananas are cooked, slit them down their length and gently open them up. Spoon some of the cream over the warm flesh and divide the remaining passion fruit pulp between the bananas – it makes the dish look just beautiful. Dust with icing sugar and serve.

These fruity barbecued kebabs are divine. Molasses isn't to everyone's taste so you could leave it out and just increase the amount of sugar, if you prefer. If you can't find tamarind paste – which is a pounded sour fruit – use extra lime juice instead.

# Tamarind and molasses-glazed fruit kebabs

Serves 4–6

1 pineapple

2 mangos, peeled and stoned (*see* page 25)

2 bananas, just underripe

seeds from 1 pomegranate

lime wedges, to serve

For the glaze

¾ tbsp tamarind paste

½ tbsp molasses

6 tbsp soft light brown sugar

finely grated zest and juice of ½ lime

1 Soak 4–6 wooden skewers in cold water for at least 30 minutes before cooking, to help prevent them from burning. Top and tail the pineapple, cut away the skin, then cut out the spiny 'eyes'. Cut lengthways into quarters, then remove and discard the hard core. Cut the pineapple into 3cm (1¼in) chunks.

2 Cut the mango into chunks about the same size as your pineapple chunks. Peel the bananas and cut into similar-sized pieces.

3 Mix the ingredients for the glaze together in a broad, shallow container and add the fruit. Turn it over in the glaze until it is well coated. Thread the fruit on to the skewers. Cook the kebabs on the barbecue over a gentle heat, otherwise the sugary glaze will burn before your fruit has softened. If they are getting too dark, wrap them in foil and return to the heat. If you prefer, you can cook them on a griddle pan or under a grill.

4 Put the cooked kebabs on to a platter and scatter over the pomegranate seeds. Serve with wedges of lime to squeeze over.

Suppa

This vegetarian dish contains cashew nuts, which I used to pick fresh off the tree in Jamaica. A single nut sits on top of the cashew fruit, so it is a prized possession; they don't grow in bags!

# Okra, cashew and tofu stir-fry

Serves 4

250g (9oz) firm tofu, cut into 2cm (¾in) dice

1 red onion, roughly chopped

1 garlic clove, finely sliced

5cm (2in) fresh root ginger, peeled and finely chopped

¼ hot red chilli (ideally Scotch Bonnet), deseeded and finely chopped

juice of 2 limes

2 tbsp soy sauce

225g (8oz) long-grain white rice

1 tbsp sunflower oil

8 okra, cut into 2cm (¾in) diagonal slices

100g (3½oz) cashew nuts

salt and black pepper, to taste

fresh coriander leaves, to garnish

1 Marinate the tofu at least an hour before you want to cook, and ideally the night before. Mix the onion, garlic, ginger, chilli, lime juice and soy sauce in a medium-sized non-reactive container. Add the tofu and gently stir to cover with the marinade; don't be too vigorous or you'll break it up. Cover and leave in the refrigerator until ready to cook, turning the tofu over in the marinade 2–3 times.

2 Pour the rice into a measuring jug, make a note of the volume, then put it in a saucepan. Add double its capacity in water. Cover and bring to the boil, then reduce the heat and simmer until it has absorbed the water and there are steam holes in the top of the rice. Turn off the heat, cover and set aside while you cook the stir-fry.

3 Take the tofu out of the marinade. Drain off the liquid and reserve. Heat the oil in a wok over a high heat. Add the onion, garlic, chilli and ginger from the marinade to the pan and stir-fry for a couple of minutes. Add the okra and continue to cook for a couple of minutes more. Tip in the nuts and fry, until they are patched with brown. Now add the tofu and very gently stir it in. Pour in the liquid from the marinade along with 200ml (7fl oz) water. Reduce the heat, cover and cook gently for 2 minutes, or until everything is heated through.

4 Taste and season if necessary. Serve with the rice and garnish with the fresh coriander leaves.

Here's a recipe that can be both summery or winter warmery!
The chillies you choose can be as mean as you like; leave the
seeds in if you dare. Serve with plain boiled rice.

# Caribbean tamarind chickpeas

Serves 6

1–2 tsp sunflower oil

1 onion, roughly chopped

1 garlic clove, finely chopped

1 bunch of fresh coriander (optional)

4cm (1½in) fresh root ginger,
peeled and finely chopped

½ butternut squash, peeled,
halved, deseeded and cut into
2.5cm (1in) cubes

1 hot red chilli (ideally Scotch
Bonnet), seeds left in or removed,
depending on how hot you like it,
finely chopped

2 × 400g cans chickpeas, drained

400g can chopped tomatoes

400ml can coconut milk

3 tsp tamarind paste

pinch of salt

pinch of sugar (optional)

1 Pour the oil into a large pan that has a lid and place over a low
heat. Add the onion and garlic and cook, stirring occasionally, for
10–15 minutes, until soft. Meanwhile, cut the stalks from the bunch
of fresh coriander into small pieces, if using. Reserve the leaves for
a garnish, if you like.

2 Put the ginger, squash, coriander stalks, chilli, rinsed chickpeas,
tomatoes, coconut milk and tamarind paste in the pan with the
softened onion and garlic. Season with a little salt; coconut is slightly
salty so you may need less than usual. Put on the lid and leave to
simmer over a low heat for 20–30 minutes, stirring occasionally.
When it is ready the squash should be tender and the flavours well
melded. Add salt, sugar or a little more tamarind paste, to taste.

3 Scatter over the fresh coriander leaves, if using, and serve.

My son Zaion devised this colourful, healthy recipe for the school dinners he makes for Thames Christian College, the school next door to our café, Papine. It's a brilliant way to get kids to eat more veg. This dish is vegetarian, but add some cooked chicken or ham, cut into strips, if you like something a bit more meaty.

# Zaion's school-dinner chow mein

Serves 4

150g (5½oz) small broccoli florets

200g (7oz) small cauliflower florets

2 carrots, cut into small batons

250g (9oz) medium egg noodles

½ tbsp sunflower oil

1 red onion, finely chopped

1 spring onion, finely chopped

1 garlic clove, finely chopped

1 red pepper, deseeded and cut into small dice

1 green pepper, deseeded and cut into small dice

2 tomatoes, cut into small dice

8 button mushrooms, quartered

1 thyme sprig

4–5 tbsp Sunshine Kit Cooking Sauce (*see* page 123)

326g can sweetcorn, drained

1–2 tbsp soy sauce

pinch of all-purpose seasoning (optional)

juice of 1 lime

1 Steam the broccoli, cauliflower and carrots until they are almost tender, then set aside. Cook the noodles according to the packet instructions, then drain.

2 Meanwhile, make the sauce. Heat the oil in a wok over a high heat, then add the red onion, spring onion and garlic and stir-fry, until softened. Add the peppers and stir-fry them, too, until softened, then add the tomatoes, mushrooms and thyme and cook, stirring, for a few minutes more. Stir in the Sunshine Kit Cooking Sauce, bring to the boil, then reduce the heat, cover, and cook for 1–2 minutes more.

3 Add the steamed vegetables and sweetcorn and cook for another minute, uncovered. Add the noodles to the pan and stir everything together. Add the soy sauce and, if you like, the all-purpose seasoning. Taste and adjust the flavours, adding more soy or Sunshine Kit Cooking Sauce, if you like. Squeeze over the lime and serve it up!

Yes, you can make pizza at home! You will need a very hot oven, preheated well in advance. Use an ordinary-sized aubergine, cut into chunks, for the topping if you can't find baby ones.

# Brixton pizza

Serves 4

15g (½oz) dried yeast

250ml (9fl oz) lukewarm water

400g (14oz) strong plain flour, plus extra for dusting the work surface

1½ tsp salt

olive oil, to oil the baking sheet, if using

For the topping

650g (1lb 7oz) butternut squash, peeled, deseeded and cut into 2cm (¾in) slices

2 red onions, cut into wedges

2 red peppers, deseeded and quartered

250g (9oz) baby aubergines, halved

2 hot red chillies (ideally Scotch Bonnet), deseeded and finely sliced

salt and black pepper

6 tbsp olive oil

2 tomatoes, halved

300g jar tomato pizza topping

150g (5½oz) baby spinach

2 × 125g packets mozzarella, drained and sliced

1 Begin by 'sponging' the yeast. Dissolve it in a small bowl with 1½ tbsp of the water and mix in 2 tbsp of the flour. Stir to make a smooth paste. Cover with a cloth and leave to rise somewhere warm for 30 minutes. Put the remaining flour in a bowl and make a well in the centre. Pour the sponge, salt and the rest of the water into the middle and mix, gradually bringing the dry ingredients into the wet ones, until you form a ball. Lightly flour your hands and a work surface and knead the dough for 10 minutes, until smooth, satiny and elastic. Transfer it to a clean bowl, cover with a cloth and leave somewhere warm for 1½ hours, or until doubled in size.

2 At least 30 minutes before baking, preheat the oven to as hot as it will go (ideally 275°C/530°F, but most ovens won't go that high). Put pizza stones or baking sheets in the oven to heat (you will transfer the pizzas on to these). Pizza stones do not need to be oiled, but the hot baking sheets should be oiled at the last minute.

3 Meanwhile, put the squash, onions, peppers and aubergines in a roasting tin, sprinkle with the chillies, season, drizzle with half the oil and roast in the hot oven for 25–30 minutes, until softened and slightly browned. Add the tomatoes for the last 5 minutes.

4 Place the dough on a lightly floured work surface and knead it again for a couple of minutes. Divide it into 4 and shape each piece into a round, about 23cm (9in) across and 1cm (½in) thick. Lay these on well-floured baking sheets from which you can transfer them easily on to the pizza stones or baking sheets in the oven.

5 Spread some tomato pizza topping over the top of each pizza and scatter over the spinach. Then place 4 slices of squash on each pizza at right angles to each other with a tomato half in the centre. Slice the peppers and lay the slices in the gaps along with the onions and aubergines. Arrange the mozzarella slices and set aside the pizzas for 10–15 minutes. Drizzle with the remaining oil, then transfer to the oven. Cook for about 12 minutes. Serve immediately.

This is one of the most popular dishes at my café. You can dub it up with chilli if you want to give it some heat; however, it's a great supper dish for kids and they may want it without the kick.

# Tuna bake

Serves 6

2 tbsp olive oil

1 onion, roughly chopped

1 red pepper, deseeded and cubed

1 green pepper, deseeded and cubed

500g (1lb 2oz) penne pasta

2 spring onions, chopped

2 × 400g cans tomatoes in thick juice

leaves from 6 thyme sprigs

salt and black pepper

2 × 200g cans tuna, drained

125g (4½oz) Cheddar cheese, grated

1 Preheat the oven to 190°C/375°F/gas mark 5. Heat the oil in a sauté pan or saucepan over a medium heat and cook the onion and peppers for 10–15 minutes, stirring occasionally, until the onion is pale gold and soft. Meanwhile, cook the pasta in plenty of boiling salted water, according to the instructions on the packet.

2 Add the spring onions to the onion and peppers and cook for another 2 minutes, then add the tomatoes and thyme. Season and bring to the boil. Simmer for about 15 minutes, or until you have a thick sauce. Stir in the tuna and heat through.

3 Drain the pasta and immediately add it to the tuna mixture. Put in most of the cheese, stir to combine, then pour the mixture into a baking dish. Sprinkle the rest of the cheese over the top and bake for 20–30 minutes, or until bubbling and golden on top.

Peter has a roadside stall, or 'Fish Stop', near Ocho Rios, on the north coast of Jamaica, where he's famous for his stuffed fish. I stopped by for lunch and loved his style. The fish was really juicy and he'd used the traditional Jamaican trick of putting crackers on top to soak the juices up, so you have a lunch-in-one. Peter uses snapper, but I've used sea bream. You could use any other robust round fish, such as sea bass.

# Peter's Fish Stop sea bream

Serves 4

4 sea bream (about 450g/1lb each), gutted and scaled

salt and black pepper

juice of 1 lime

250g (9oz) red cabbage, shredded

8 okra, cut into 1cm (½in) diagonal slices

½ red onion, finely sliced

8 thick water biscuits or crackers

For the seasoning

2.5cm (1in) fresh root ginger, peeled and roughly chopped

1 garlic clove

leaves from 4 large thyme sprigs

4 spring onions, green parts only, roughly chopped

1 hot red chilli (ideally Scotch Bonnet), deseeded and finely chopped

1 tbsp cider vinegar

1 tbsp olive oil

1 Preheat the oven to 200°C/400°F/gas mark 6. Wash the sea bream inside and outside, then pat dry with kitchen paper. Place each fish on a large piece of foil, big enough to wrap around it. Season the inside of each fish thoroughly and squeeze the lime juice over the fish.

2 Divide the cabbage, okra and red onion between the fish and stuff into the cavity of each. Don't worry if the stuffing spills out into the foil parcel. Slash the top of each fish 3 times, on the diagonal.

3 Put all the seasoning ingredients in the bowl of a small food processor and add 5 tbsp water. Whizz up to get a semi-smooth paste. Slather this inside and over the top of the sea bream, then place the water biscuits or crackers on top.

4 Wrap the fish in their individual foil parcels and cook in the oven for 30–40 minutes, until the flesh is cooked through (it should be opaque at the thickest part). Serve just as it is, in the foil.

My, this is a good dish! Use it as a kind of blueprint and use any vegetables you like, such as ordinary potatoes, courgettes, tomatoes or aubergines. It's quick, too; supper can be on the table in 30 minutes. Serve it with plain boiled rice.

# Chicken, pepper and squash curry

Serves 4

1 tbsp groundnut oil

2 onions, sliced

1 red pepper, deseeded and cubed

1 green pepper, deseeded and cubed

1 red chilli, deseeded and finely sliced

2cm (¾in) fresh root ginger, peeled and finely chopped

4 tsp curry powder

1 tsp ground coriander

2 tsp ground turmeric

325ml (11fl oz) canned coconut cream

1½ tbsp soft light brown sugar

1 bay leaf

8 bone-in chicken thighs, skin removed

600g (1lb 5oz) squash, peeled, deseeded and cut into 3–4cm (1¼–1½in) cubes

salt and black pepper

fresh coriander leaves, to serve (optional)

1 Heat the oil in a large pan and cook the onions and peppers over a medium heat for 10–15 minutes, until the onion is pale gold and soft. Add the chilli, ginger and spices and cook for another minute, stirring a little. Add the coconut cream plus 160ml (5½fl oz) water, the sugar and bay leaf. Cut each chicken thigh in half by positioning a heavy knife on the chicken and whacking it with a rolling pin, and add to the stew. Bring to just under the boil, then reduce the heat to medium and cook for 15 minutes without a lid.

2 Add the squash to the stew. Cook for another 12 minutes, or until the chicken is cooked through (pierce the thickest piece of chicken with a skewer – if the juices run clear, it is done; if not, give it another 5 minutes, then test again), and the squash is soft.

3 To thicken the stew, press some of the squash with the back of a wooden spoon so that it breaks up. Season to taste and serve, sprinkled with fresh coriander leaves, if you like.

This Cuban recipe uses a *sofrito* – in this case a mixture of onion, garlic, tomato and pepper – with some succulent chicken pieces to make a delicious casserole. Serve it with couscous or rice and green vegetables or salad.

# Havana chicken

Serves 4

4 tbsp sunflower oil

1 onion, finely chopped

3 garlic cloves, finely chopped

4 tomatoes

½ red pepper, deseeded and cut into 2cm (¾in) dice

salt and black pepper

½ tsp ground cumin

1 oregano sprig

125ml (4fl oz) white wine or water

4 bone-in chicken breast pieces with wings, skin left on

1 Heat half the oil in a large casserole dish that has a lid over a medium heat and add the onion and garlic. Cook, stirring occasionally, for about 5 minutes, or until softened.

2 Meanwhile, peel the tomatoes: cut a cross in the bottom of each and put them in a bowl. Pour over just-boiled water to cover and leave for 30 seconds, then transfer to a bowl of cold water. The skin should slide off. Peel and roughly chop.

3 Add the pepper to the onion and garlic in the casserole dish and cook, stirring occasionally, for another couple of minutes. Add the tomatoes and cook further, until the water starts to evaporate and the sauce thickens slightly. Season well, then add the cumin, oregano and wine or water. Simmer for 4–5 minutes to reduce slightly. Adjust the seasoning to taste.

4 While the sauce is cooking, pour the remaining oil into a frying pan over a high heat. Brown the chicken on both sides, then add it to the *sofrito*. Put on the lid and cook for 20–30 minutes, or until the chicken is cooked (pierce the thickest piece of chicken with a skewer – if the juices run clear, it is done; if not, give it another 5 minutes, then test again), stirring occasionally to ensure it doesn't catch on the bottom.

This is a good supper dish, I've been told, that reheats really well. Be sure to taste it as you are making it; you want to get the balance of sweet and sour just right. For the dried fruit, a mixture of mango, pineapple, papaya and apple is good. Serve with plain boiled rice and a green vegetable such as spinach or French beans.

# Sweet and sour pork with tropical fruits

Serves 6

2 tbsp sunflower oil

750g (1lb 10oz) braising pork, such as pork shoulder, diced into cubes about 3cm (1¼in) square

2 onions, roughly chopped

2 leeks, cut into 2.5cm (1in) slices

1 celery stick, finely chopped

1 red chilli, deseeded and finely chopped

2.5cm (1in) fresh root ginger, peeled and grated

250g (9oz) mixed tropical dried fruit, such as mango, pineapple and papaya

1½ tbsp plain flour

500ml (18fl oz) chicken stock

1 tbsp cider vinegar

2 tbsp soy sauce

4 thyme sprigs

2 bay leaves

salt and black pepper

soft brown sugar (optional)

1 Heat the oil in a heavy-based casserole dish over a medium heat. Add the pork and cook, stirring, until coloured all over. Remove from the pan and set aside. In the same pan cook the onions and leeks for around 12–15 minutes, until soft and pale golden. Add the celery, chilli, ginger and dried fruit and cook for a couple of minutes more, then return the pork, with any juices that have run out of it, to the casserole. Stir in the flour and cook for another minute; this will help to thicken the casserole. Add the stock and bring to the boil, then give it a good stir and reduce the heat to a simmer. Add the vinegar, soy sauce, thyme and bay leaves, then season.

2 Simmer, uncovered, over a low heat for about 1½ hours, by which time the pork should be very tender. Taste carefully to get the sweet and sour balance right. Add more vinegar or soy sauce if it is too sweet or, if you think it isn't sweet enough (though that would be surprising with all that fruit!), add a little soft brown sugar.

No, we don't have shepherd's pie in Jamaica, but it is a great family supper and I wanted to give you a dubbed-up version. There is no chilli in this as children don't always want much heat, but if it's for adults (or brave children), then stick in a Scotch Bonnet, too. I have brought something of my Scottish heritage to this by adding oats. This is healthy and economical as it bulks out the meat. Give this to your little angels and they will never want the English version again!

# Caribbean spiced shepherd's pie

Serves 6

2 tbsp olive oil

750g (1lb 10oz) minced lamb

2 onions, roughly chopped

3 carrots, diced

3 garlic cloves, finely chopped

1 tsp ground cumin

1 tsp ground mixed spice

1 tsp ground cinnamon

300ml (½ pint) chicken or lamb stock, or water

finely grated zest and juice of 1 orange

6 tbsp tomato purée

3 tsp soft dark brown sugar

20g (¾oz) rolled porridge oats

salt and black pepper

1 tbsp chopped fresh coriander or parsley, to serve (optional)

For the sweet potato topping

1kg (2lb 4oz) sweet potatoes

35g (1¼oz) butter

1 Heat the oil in a large, broad casserole dish over a high heat and brown the minced lamb. You may need to do this in batches, as putting too much meat in the pan will make it sweat instead of fry. Transfer the browned lamb to a bowl.

2 In the same pan, cook the onions and carrots, until the onions are pale gold and soft. Add the garlic and spices and cook for another minute. Return the lamb to the pan, then add the stock or water, orange zest and juice, tomato purée, sugar and oats. Season, bring to the boil, then reduce the heat and cook, uncovered and stirring from time to time, for 45 minutes to 1 hour. The stock should reduce so that you have a good thick mixture. If it seems too dry, add more stock or water.

3 Meanwhile, make your sweet potato topping. Preheat the oven to 190°C/375°F/gas mark 5. Set the sweet potatoes on a baking sheet and bake them in their skins; they will take about 40 minutes to become tender, depending on their size. When they're soft, slit them down the middle and scoop the flesh into a bowl. Mash it with half the butter and some salt and pepper.

4 Spoon the lamb into a pie dish and spread the sweet potato on top, roughing it up with a fork to give it an attractive, uneven surface. Dot with the rest of the butter. Return to the oven and cook for 20 minutes, or until golden and bubbling up at the edges. Scatter with coriander or parsley before serving, if you like.

My son Zaion runs our café, Papine, in Battersea, London. Next-door is a small, innovative private school, Thames Christian College. The headteacher wanted the kids to eat freshly prepared school dinners and there we were, right on the doorstep. Zaion works with the school to provide dishes that are a hit with all ages. This is my version of his school dinner spaghetti bolognese, here for four or five people rather than 40! Let me tell you, it's quite a different story to the school dinners I ate as a boy...

# Zaion's seasoned-up spaghetti bolognese

Serves 4–5

1 tbsp vegetable oil

1 onion, finely chopped

1 spring onion, green part only, finely chopped

1 garlic clove, finely chopped

1 red pepper, deseeded and cut into small dice

1 yellow pepper, deseeded and cut into small dice

400g (14oz) minced beef

8 button mushrooms, cut into small dice

1 thyme sprig

400g can tomatoes

2 tbsp tomato purée

2 tbsp tomato ketchup

100ml (3½fl oz) Sunshine Kit Cooking Sauce (see page 123)

salt and black pepper

400–500g (14oz–1lb 2oz) spaghetti

grated Parmesan cheese, to serve

1 Heat half the oil in a large pan and gently fry the onion, spring onion and garlic for about 10 minutes, stirring occasionally, until softened. Add the peppers and cook, stirring occasionally, until softened. Transfer the vegetables to a bowl and set aside.

2 Pour the rest of the oil into the pan. Add the mince and brown over a medium-high heat, stirring from time to time. (If you want to make this dish more quickly, just add the mince directly to the cooked vegetables in the pan; browning it just gives it a little more flavour.) Return the vegetables to the pan and stir in along with the mushrooms, thyme, tomatoes, tomato purée, tomato ketchup and the Sunshine Kit Cooking Sauce.

3 Cover and cook over a low heat for 30 minutes. Adjust the seasoning to taste.

4 Cook the spaghetti in plenty of boiling, salted water, following the instructions on the packet, then drain. Divide the pasta between 4 or 5 warmed plates, spoon over the meat sauce and sprinkle generously with the grated Parmesan.

Soufflés are not as hard to make as you'd think. Try this and you'll see. You could use half Cheddar cheese and half Parmesan cheese for this recipe if you want a different sort of flavour. Serve with steamed peas or a green salad.

# Sweet potato and Parmesan soufflé

Serves 4

50g (1¾oz) butter, plus extra for the dish

400g (14oz) sweet potato, peeled and cut into 2cm (¾in) dice

50g (1¾oz) plain flour

a little hot water or milk, if necessary

salt and black pepper

6 large eggs, separated

175g (6oz) Parmesan cheese, grated

1 Preheat the oven to 200°C/400°F/gas mark 6 and put a baking sheet inside to heat up. Butter a 1.25 litre (2 pint) soufflé dish.

2 Put the sweet potato in a saucepan of water, bring to the boil, then reduce the heat to a simmer, cover and cook for about 5 minutes, until tender. Drain the sweet potato, transferring the cooking water to another pan and keeping it simmering. Mash the sweet potato to a rough purée.

3 Melt the butter in the pan in which you cooked the potato and stir in the flour. Cook, stirring constantly, for a couple of minutes. Measure 350ml (12fl oz) of the cooking water (adding a little extra hot water or milk to make up the amount, if necessary) and gradually stir it into the flour and butter mixture. Keep stirring, over a low heat, until thick. Stir the mashed sweet potato into the sauce and season well, then add the egg yolks and cheese. Pour the mixture into a large bowl. Discard any remaining cooking water.

4 In another clean bowl, whisk the egg whites until they form stiff peaks. Gently mix a spoonful of this into the sweet potato mixture, then carefully fold in the rest of the egg white, keeping as much air in the mixture as possible. Scrape it into the soufflé dish, then place on the hot baking sheet in the oven and cook for 45 minutes.

This recipe comes from a talented Caribbean chef, Christian Ghisays of the Royal Plantation hotel in Ocho Rios in Jamaica. Christian says you may adjust the amount of chilli according to taste – Jamaicans love it but, he warns, it may be too much for those not used to the heat!

# Lime-escovitched sea bream with tiger prawns

Serves 4

80ml (2½fl oz) lime juice

50ml (2fl oz) cider vinegar

½ hot red chilli (ideally red or yellow Scotch Bonnet), deseeded and finely sliced

small pinch of ground allspice

pinch of caster sugar

2 carrots, cut into long batons

12 okra, cut into 1cm (½in) diagonal slices

1 small red onion, finely sliced

1 lime, finely sliced, with a quarter-segment removed from each slice

salt and black pepper

4 × sea bream fillets (450g/1lb in total)

1 tsp sunflower oil

20g (¾oz) butter

16 cooked, peeled tiger prawns

2 small courgettes (ideally 1 green and 1 yellow), sliced into long batons

1 Bring 150ml (5fl oz) water to the boil and add the lime juice, vinegar, chilli, allspice and sugar. Stir well. Add the carrots, okra and red onion and boil for about 3 minutes to part-cook the vegetables and reduce the liquid slightly, then turn off the heat. Add the lime slices and stir.

2 Season the sea bream fillets on both sides. Heat the oil and half the butter in a frying pan over a high heat. Cook the fish, skin-side down, for 2 minutes. Turn the fish over and add the prawns. Continue to cook, giving the prawns a stir so they heat up all the way through, until the fish is cooked through.

3 Meanwhile, bring a small pan of water to the boil and blanch the courgettes for 2 minutes, then drain. Reheat the lime escovitch sauce, if necessary. If you want to make it more glossy, stir in the remaining butter.

4 Arrange the courgettes on warmed serving plates, then place a fish fillet on top. Spoon the prawns and vegetables over the top and around the plate. Arrange the lime slices, carrots and onions for colour. Enjoy!

Serves 8

1 whole salmon (about 2.5kg/
5lb 8oz), cleaned and gutted

1½ tbsp olive oil

For the stuffing

50g (1¾oz) raisins

50g (1¾oz) dried mango

1½ tbsp olive oil

50g (1¾oz) butter

1 onion, finely chopped

2.5cm (1in) fresh root ginger,
peeled and finely chopped

1 red chilli, deseeded and
finely sliced

6 spring onions, chopped

3 garlic cloves, finely chopped

leaves from 3 thyme sprigs

1 piece of preserved stem ginger
in syrup, finely chopped

½ tsp ground cinnamon

25g (1oz) chopped almonds

500g (1lb 2oz) spinach, washed
and thick stalks removed

75g (2¾oz) fresh white breadcrumbs

salt and black pepper

finely grated zest of 1 lime,
plus the juice of ½ lime

lime wedges, to serve (optional)

This is a wonderful Christmas centrepiece. It's a very impressive-looking dish, and contains a delicious mixture of sweet and savoury flavours. The combination of spinach and mango may seem odd, but it really works.

# My baked Christmas fish

1 First make the stuffing. Put the raisins and mango in a small bowl and cover with just-boiled water from the kettle. Leave to soak for 30 minutes, then drain. Preheat the oven to 180°C/350°F/gas mark 4.

2 Heat the oil and half the butter in a large frying pan and sauté the onion over a medium heat until soft and pale gold. Add the fresh ginger, chilli, spring onions and garlic and cook for another 2 minutes. Add the thyme, preserved ginger and cinnamon and cook for another couple of minutes. Transfer the mixture to a bowl and add the soaked fruit and almonds.

3 Put the spinach in a large pan with the water that is left clinging to the leaves after washing. Cover and set over a low heat. Cook for 4 minutes, or until wilted, turning the leaves over halfway through. Leave until cool enough to handle, then squeeze the excess water out with your hands and roughly chop. Add the spinach to the rest of the stuffing along with the breadcrumbs. Season really well and add the lime zest and juice, and finally the rest of the butter, cut into small dice. Mix together with your hands.

4 Place the salmon on a large roasting tin or baking sheet lined with foil. You may need to curl it to fit. Rub inside and out with the oil and seasoning. Pack all the stuffing inside, then season the top of the fish. Pull the foil up around the salmon so that it is enclosed in a kind of tent – don't wrap it closely round its body – then scrunch the foil together to make a sealed package. Place in the oven (it may be a squeeze; don't worry if the fish overhangs the roasting tin or baking sheet, just make sure it doesn't touch the sides of the oven) and cook for 45 minutes, pulling the foil back so the fish can colour on top after 30 minutes. Now check the fish: the eye should be completely white and the flesh near the bone at the thickest part should not look glassy. If it isn't fully cooked, return to the oven and cook for another 4 minutes before checking again. Serve with lime wedges, if liked.

Serves 4

1 whole chicken
(about 1.2kg/2lb 12oz)

300g (10½oz) pumpkin or butternut
squash, peeled, deseeded and cut
into 4cm (1½in) chunks

200g (7oz) potatoes, cut into 3cm
(1¼in) chunks

½ chicken stock cube (optional)

salt and black pepper

lime wedges, to serve (optional)

For the stuffing

½ red onion, roughly chopped

1 spring onion, roughly chopped

3cm (1¼in) fresh root ginger,
peeled and finely chopped

2 tbsp finely chopped fresh
coriander leaves

½ hot red chilli (ideally Scotch
Bonnet), deseeded and finely
chopped

1 large rosemary sprig

1 bay leaf

2 garlic cloves, roughly chopped

2 good pinches of black pepper

good pinch of salt

My mother makes the best chicken soup in the world. Here's my own spin on it...if that's allowed, Mum! It's as much a stew as a soup, a chunky dish that is a meal in itself.

# Inside-out chicken supper

1 Mix together all the ingredients for the stuffing in a bowl. Spoon the stuffing into the chicken, then put the bird in a casserole dish that is just large enough to hold it. Add the pumpkin or squash and the potatoes. Pour over about 850ml (1½ pints) water, or enough to almost cover the chicken. If you want to add a bit more flavour, crumble in the stock cube at this point, but it's not at all crucial.

2 Put a lid on the casserole dish and bring to the boil over a high heat. Reduce the heat to medium-low and simmer for about 1 hour, or until cooked through (pierce the thickest piece of chicken with a skewer – if the juices run clear, it is done; if not, give it another 5 minutes, then test again). The meat should be tender and coming away from the bone easily.

3 Carefully take the chicken out of the pot, draining any liquid and loose stuffing back into the casserole dish. Use a carving knife and fork to cut the chicken into 4 or 8 pieces: 2 breast meat and wing and 2 leg and thigh (split each in half for 8 pieces). Taste the liquid in the pot and adjust the seasoning if necessary.

4 Put the chicken pieces in large bowls and spoon over the vegetables and soup. If you like, serve with wedges of lime.

Serves 4

1.4kg (3lb 4oz) butterflied
leg of lamb

For the marinade

2cm (¾in) fresh root ginger,
peeled and grated

½ tbsp black peppercorns

1 hot red chilli (ideally Scotch
Bonnet), deseeded and finely
chopped

good handful of mint leaves

leaves from 4 thyme sprigs

½ tsp ground allspice

2 garlic cloves, roughly chopped

1 tsp coriander seeds

generous grating of nutmeg

1 tbsp runny honey

2 tbsp olive oil

For the vegetables

500g (1lb 2oz) small, waxy potatoes

2 sweet potatoes, cut into large
chunks, about 4cm (1½in) square

3 large carrots, cut into large
chunks, about 4cm (1½in) square

2 large onions, cut into wedges

4 thyme sprigs

2 tbsp olive oil

salt and black pepper

This is one of my favourite recipes in the whole book. Look how quickly you can cook roast lamb if you get your butcher to butterfly a leg for you (he takes the bone out and leaves you with a big flat piece that's easy to carve). Reduce the amount of chilli (or leave it out) if you're cooking for guests with delicate palates. Sunday lunch never tasted so good!

# My hot hot lamb with roast roots

1 Lay the lamb out flat in a roasting tin. Pierce the fleshy side all over with a sharp knife. Put all the ingredients for the marinade, except the honey and oil, in a mortar and grind into a paste with the pestle. Stir in the honey and oil. Spread this marinade all over the lamb, working into the slits you made. Cover and put in the refrigerator to marinate for between 1 and 24 hours. Turn the lamb over every so often. When you're ready to cook, preheat the oven to 220°C/425°F/gas mark 7.

2 Put the vegetables in a roasting tin and toss with the thyme and oil, then season. Place a rack over these and set the lamb – fat side up – on top. Roast for 15 minutes, then reduce the heat to 190°C/375°F/ gas mark 5 and cook for a further 20–25 minutes (20 will give you pink lamb) until cooked through. Shake the vegetables a couple of times during cooking to make sure they're getting coated in the lamb roasting juices, and baste the lamb every so often with these juices.

3 When done, remove the lamb from the oven, cover with foil and insulate with a dish cloth. Leave for 15 minutes so the meat can rest. Carve the lamb and serve with the roasted vegetables.

Serves 4

2 tsp Dijon mustard

4 × 200g (7oz) racks of lamb, trimmed

4 tsp finely chopped rosemary leaves

1 tbsp olive oil

For the sauce

1 tbsp olive oil

1 red onion, finely chopped

1 garlic clove, finely chopped

18 fresh or preserved cherries, stoned and quartered

400ml (14fl oz) lamb or beef stock

2 tbsp rum

1 tsp soy sauce

salt and black pepper

couple of mint sprigs, finely chopped

To serve

steamed French beans

16 fresh or preserved cherries, stoned

fresh coriander leaves

4 small rosemary sprigs

I was given this recipe by Christian Ghisays, the chef at the Royal Plantation hotel in Ocho Rios on the beautiful north coast of Jamaica. Christian loves the natural produce of the island and in this recipe cooks cherries (he uses wild ones) with lamb. Serve the dish with a green vegetable, such as French beans.

# Lamb with cherry and rum sauce

1 Preheat the oven to 220°C/425°F/gas mark 7. To make the sauce, heat the oil in a saucepan and add the onion and garlic. Cook over a medium-low heat for 3–4 minutes, stirring often, until softened. Add half the cherries and all the stock and let the sauce simmer for 5 minutes. Add the rum and boil hard to reduce the liquid by half. Add the remaining cherries and the soy sauce, then season and add the mint. Set aside.

2 Spread the mustard over the lamb and rub with salt and pepper, then pat on the rosemary. Heat the oil in an ovenproof frying pan and sear the meat for about 3 minutes each side, then transfer to the oven for 6–7 minutes, until cooked but still pink inside. When cooked through, remove from the oven, cover with foil and allow to rest for a couple of minutes. Meanwhile, reheat the sauce.

3 Make a bed of steamed French beans on 4 serving plates, then cut the lamb into cutlets and fan them out on top of the beans. Spoon around the sauce and garnish with the cherries, fresh coriander and rosemary sprigs.

Try this for Sunday lunch and your family will be knocked out.
It is one of the tastiest pork dishes ever, I am told, and eating it
cold in sandwiches is almost as good.

# Cuban roast pork

Serves 6–8

1 tbsp cumin seeds

½ tbsp black peppercorns

6 garlic cloves

1 tbsp dried oregano

pinch of salt

juice of 1 orange

juice of 2 limes

25ml (1fl oz) sherry

2 tbsp olive oil

1.8kg (4lb) shoulder of pork, trimmed

Sautéed Sweet Potatoes with Thyme, to serve (*see* page 116)

1 Heat a small, heavy pan over a medium heat. Add the cumin and peppercorns and stir constantly for 2 minutes, or until fragrant and beginning to brown, then cool. Using a mortar and pestle, crush the toasted spices with the garlic, oregano and salt to make a paste. (You can also do this in the bowl of a small food processor.)

2 Transfer the spice mixture to a small bowl, and stir in the orange and lime juice, sherry and oil. Pierce the pork all over with a sharp knife and place it in a large resealable plastic bag, then pour the marinade over the meat and seal the bag. Refrigerate for between 12 and 24 hours, turning the bag over occasionally.

3 When ready to cook, preheat the oven to 200°C/400°F/gas mark 6. Put the pork in a roasting tin (reserve the marinade) and cook for about 30 minutes, then reduce the heat to 160°C/ 325°F/gas mark 3 and roast for another 2 hours, regularly basting the pork with the pan juices and the leftover marinade, until cooked through.

4 Transfer the pork to a carving board, cover loosely with foil and leave to rest for 15 minutes. Pour the cooking juices into a saucepan and skim the fat off the top. Bring to the boil, then simmer for 5 minutes. Carve the pork and serve with the reduced juices, accompanied by my Sautéed Sweet Potatoes with Thyme.

This is a warming dish using a favourite Caribbean ingredient: stout. If you aren't familiar with dumplings you are in for a treat – they are delicious, and easy to make. You don't need potatoes or rice with this; just green vegetables! If you'd rather bake the dumplings, add them to the casserole (replacing the lid) for the last 10–15 minutes of cooking time, until they are well risen and cooked through.

# Beef and carrots in stout with Levi's twister dumplings

Serves 4–6

3 tbsp groundnut or sunflower oil, plus extra for deep-frying (optional)

1kg (2lb 4oz) braising beef, cut into large chunks, about 4cm (1½in) square

700g (1lb 9oz) mixed onions, celery and carrots, cut into large chunks

330ml bottle stout

salt and black pepper

For the dumplings

225g (8oz) self-raising flour, plus extra to dust

1 tsp salt

1 tsp baking powder

4 tbsp demerara sugar

1 Preheat the oven to 160°C/325°F/gas mark 3. Heat 2 tbsp of the oil in an ovenproof casserole dish over a high heat and brown the meat in batches on all sides. Remove the meat and any juices and set aside. Add the remaining oil to the casserole dish and fry the vegetables over a medium heat for about 10 minutes until very lightly coloured (be sure not to burn them). Add the stout and stir to scrape up all the flavour from the bottom of the dish. Pour in 500ml (18fl oz) water, return the meat to the dish and season. Bring to the boil, then immediately reduce the heat.

2 Cover the casserole and cook in the oven for 2 hours 15 minutes. Check a couple of times during cooking to make sure the mixture hasn't become too dry, and add more water if necessary. If there is too much liquid, leave the lid off for the last 30 minutes of cooking.

3 Meanwhile, to make the dumplings, sift the flour, salt and baking powder into a bowl. Add the sugar. Now gradually mix in up to 150ml (5fl oz) water until you have a good dough: it should be soft but not sticky. Turn it out on to a floured surface and knead for about 10 minutes, until smooth. Break off pieces of dough and roll them into sausage shapes, each about 15cm (6in) long. Now tie each roll into a twist (make a loose knot in it). Set on a floured baking sheet.

4 To deep-fry the dumplings, pour enough oil into a large saucepan to come halfway up the sides, then place it over a medium heat until the temperature on a cook's thermometer reaches 190°C/ 375°F, or until a little nugget of the dough goes pale gold in about 45 seconds when dropped into the oil. Deep-fry all the twisters, about 3 at a time, for about 5 minutes, or until golden and cooked through (pull one apart to test for doneness). Blot any excess oil on kitchen paper and serve with the hot stew.

On the Side

Here are a pair of Caribbean twists on a classic dish: use sweet potatoes instead of what we Jamaicans call 'Irish potatoes', and add some thyme.

# Sautéed sweet potatoes with thyme

Serves 4

4 sweet potatoes, peeled and cut into 3cm (1¼in) dice

salt and black pepper

25g (1oz) butter

2 tbsp olive oil

2 garlic cloves

6 thyme sprigs

1 Put the sweet potatoes in a large saucepan of salted water. Bring to the boil, reduce the heat and simmer for 5 minutes, then drain.

2 Heat the butter and oil in a large frying pan over a low heat until the butter has melted. Add the sweet potatoes, garlic and thyme. Cook over a medium-low heat for 10–15 minutes, turning the potatoes over after 5 minutes or so, and then again after another 5 minutes, until they are crisp and tender.

3 Season well and serve immediately.

This is so much better than all that stodgy stuff you find on buffets every summer. Add lime to the dressing if it's your thing.

# Levi's herbed potato salad

Serves 4

500g (1lb 2oz) waxy new potatoes, halved or quartered, depending on size

25ml (1fl oz) warm chicken stock

salt and black pepper

4 generous tbsp mayonnaise

2 tbsp Greek yogurt

3 tbsp finely chopped parsley or fresh coriander

1 Put the potatoes in a saucepan and cover with water. Bring to the boil and cook for 15 minutes, or until tender. Drain, then return to the pan and immediately add the chicken stock, season and stir. Leave the potatoes to sit and absorb the stock while they cool.

2 When the potatoes have reached room temperature, add the mayonnaise, yogurt and herbs and stir to combine. Adjust the seasoning to taste.

Deep purple and scented with ginger, this is my special version of red cabbage. It's a delicious accompaniment to Christmas lunch or any autumn and winter meals.

# Levi's sticky red cabbage

Serves 6

60g (2¼oz) dried mango

15g (½oz) butter

1 red onion, finely sliced

1 red cabbage (about 1.1kg/2lb 7oz), quartered, cored and shredded

100ml (3½fl oz) cider vinegar

5 tbsp light muscovado sugar

3 pieces of preserved stem ginger in syrup, finely chopped, plus 2 tbsp stem ginger syrup

3 thyme sprigs

2 bay leaves

salt and black pepper

juice of 1 lime, to serve (optional)

1 Place the mango in a small bowl, cover with just-boiled water from the kettle and leave to soak for 20 minutes, then cut into strips. Meanwhile, melt the butter in a casserole dish that has a lid. Add the red onion and cook over a medium heat, stirring often, until softened. Add the cabbage and stir again. Add the rest of the ingredients, except for the lime, seasoning to taste. Stir well, cover and cook over a low heat for 45 minutes, stirring every so often.

2 Take the lid off the pan and continue to cook until most of the liquid has evaporated and the cabbage is tender.

3 Adjust the seasoning and the sweet-sour factor to taste, adding a little more cider vinegar if it is too sweet, or a little more sugar if it is too sour. Squeeze a little lime juice over the top to add a fresh layer to the flavours, if you like.

I like the long, tapered, sweet piquillo peppers that are now quite widely available. However, if you can't find any, use ordinary red peppers. Here, I've dubbed them up with some Caribbean flavourings and topped them with melting mozzarella cheese.

# Stuffed piquillo peppers

Serves 4 as a side dish or starter,
2 as a main course

4 piquillo peppers

90g (3¼oz) couscous

3 tbsp finely chopped fresh coriander leaves

2 spring onions, green parts only, finely chopped

juice of 1 lime

salt and black pepper

150g (5½oz) mozzarella cheese, cut into small dice

1 Preheat the oven to 180°C/350°F/gas mark 4. Trim the peppers by cutting out the green stalk and scraping out the seeds through the stalk hole. Rinse the insides with water. Place the peppers on a baking sheet and roast for 30 minutes, until soft. Cool a little, then cut in half and carefully peel off the skin, keeping the halves intact so they can be stuffed.

2 Meanwhile, soak the couscous in 200ml (7fl oz) just-boiled water for 10 minutes. Add the coriander, spring onion and lime juice, and stir to combine. Season with pepper and a very small amount of salt.

3 Stuff the peppers with the couscous, then put them back on the baking sheet and dot with the mozzarella. Grind over a little more pepper and return to the oven for another 15 minutes, until the couscous has heated through and the mozzarella has melted.

This delicious sauce goes well with my Coconut King Prawns (*see* page 60) or alongside a beautiful piece of salmon or some fried chicken.

# Mango fruity sauce

Serves 6–8
as a dip

1 ripe mango, peeled, stoned and roughly chopped (*see* page 25)

20g (¾oz) fresh coriander leaves

2 spring onions, green parts only

4 tbsp Greek yogurt

salt and black pepper

1 Put all the ingredients in a blender or food processor and whizz until smooth.

2 Adjust the seasoning to taste. Pour the sauce into a small bowl, cover with clingfilm and keep in the refrigerator until needed. Eat within a couple of days.

My Sunshine Kit of Caribbean flavourings includes heat (chilli, black pepper and ginger) and fragrance (nutmeg and thyme). This sauce is a useful standby full of the Sunshine Kit ingredients. You can have it handy in the refrigerator to add to dishes such as Zaion's School-dinner Chow Mein (*see* page 85) and Zaion's Seasoned-up Spaghetti Bolognese (*see* page 96).

# Sunshine kit cooking sauce

Makes about 450ml (16fl oz)

400g can tomatoes

1 tbsp tomato purée

1 garlic clove, roughly chopped

2 spring onions, green parts only, roughly chopped

1 hot red chilli (ideally Scotch Bonnet), seeds left in or removed depending on how hot you like it, roughly chopped

leaves from 2 thyme sprigs

50g (1¾oz) fresh coriander leaves and stalks

1 tsp black pepper

good grating of nutmeg (about ½–1 tsp)

1 tsp ground ginger

¾ tsp ground allspice

¾ tsp ground cinnamon

5 tbsp dark muscovado sugar

2 tbsp cider vinegar

1½ tsp salt, or to taste

1 Put all the ingredients in a blender or food processor. Whizz to get everything mixed together nice and smooth. Taste and adjust the flavours as you like, adding a bit more cider vinegar, sugar or salt if you want to adjust the acidity, sweetness or saltiness, and adjust the spices if necessary to get a flavour to your liking.

2 Pour the sauce into a saucepan, bring to the boil, then reduce the heat and simmer for 5 minutes. Adjust the seasoning to taste once more, if necessary.

3 Pour the sauce into a small bowl, allow to cool, cover with clingfilm and keep in the refrigerator until needed. It's best eaten within a week – that shouldn't be a problem, it's so delicious!

Here's a great Cuban dish that I've named after the iconic revolutionary, Che Guevara. I've also tried making the chips with ripe bananas instead of plantain, and left out the salt and served them on vanilla ice cream – fantastic! Serve with drinks.

# Che chips

Serves 4–6

sunflower oil, for deep-frying

2 ripe plantains, peeled and cut diagonally into 1cm (½in) slices

salt, to sprinkle

1 Pour enough oil into a large saucepan to come halfway up the sides. Heat the oil until the temperature on a cook's thermometer reaches 190°C/375°F or a small nugget of plantain goes pale gold in about 45 seconds when dropped into the oil.

2 Working in batches, deep-fry the plantain pieces, turning them over once or twice while cooking. They will take 3–6 minutes in total. Do not crowd the pan or they will take longer to cook.

3 Drain the chips on kitchen paper to remove any excess oil and sprinkle with salt.

This stuff is fabulocious with pork chops or cooked ham. It may be a tropical preserve, but why not make a jar for Christmas and see how it cheers up cold meats? You will need a jam jar.

# Spiced pickled pineapple

Makes 400g (14oz)

1 ripe pineapple

200ml (7fl oz) cider vinegar

350g (12oz) caster sugar

2 star anise

1 piece of preserved stem ginger in syrup, finely sliced

1 small red chilli, deseeded and finely sliced

1 onion, very finely sliced

1 To sterilise the jam jar, place it in a large saucepan and cover with cold water. Bring to the boil and simmer for 10–15 minutes. Remove from the water and leave upside down to dry.

2 Top and tail the pineapple. Cut away the skin, then cut out the spiny 'eyes'. Cut into rounds. Halve the rounds, remove the hard core from each piece, then cut into small irregular shapes (you don't want to end up with something that looks like canned pineapple chunks).

3 Put the vinegar and sugar in a saucepan and bring to the boil, stirring every so often to help the sugar dissolve. Add the star anise, ginger and chilli and simmer for 10 minutes, then add the onion and cook for another 10 minutes, until the onion has softened and the mixture thickened.

4 Add the pineapple and simmer for a further 10 minutes, or until the juice is quite syrupy (it will thicken more as it cools) and the pineapple is tender. Transfer immediately to the hot, sterilised jam jar, and seal. Keep the Spiced Pickled Pineapple until needed: it will keep for about 6 months, but should be refrigerated once opened.

This is the best chutney ever – trust me! It's hot with chilli and warm with ginger. I can eat it on bread just as it is but it's also fab in a cheese sandwich and with spicy roast meat or chicken. You will need two jam jars.

# Mango and ginger chutney

Makes 500g
(1lb 2oz)

350g (12oz) onion, finely chopped

400ml (14fl oz) distilled malt vinegar

2 bay leaves

2 red chillies, deseeded and finely chopped

2 green chillies, deseeded and finely chopped

1 tsp black mustard seeds

1kg (2lb 4oz) mangos, peeled, stoned and sliced into wedges (*see* page 25)

250g (9oz) tart apples, peeled and sliced

450g (1lb) granulated sugar

2 tsp ground ginger

¼ tsp ground cloves

½ tsp ground allspice

1 Put the onions in a large saucepan with the vinegar, bay leaves and chillies and simmer over a low heat for 10 minutes, or until they are almost tender. Meanwhile, toast the mustard seeds under a medium grill until they begin to pop.

2 Add the mangos, apples and mustard seeds to the onion mixture and cook for about 15 minutes, or until the fruit is soft. Add the sugar, ginger, cloves and allspice, increase the heat, and boil for 30–40 minutes, or until the mixture resembles a thick jam. Stir occasionally to avoid sticking. Allow to cool, then serve.

3 Alternatively, spoon into sterilised jars while still hot, and seal (*see* page 125 for sterilising instructions). The chutney will keep for up to 9 months, but should be refrigerated once opened.

A lovely dish with good colour and gentle spicing, this is my dub-it-up take on a classic Indian favourite, pilau rice. Make an even more Caribbean version by using callalloo instead of spinach, if you like.

# Roots' rice

Serves 6

250g (9oz) basmati rice

2 tbsp sunflower or groundnut oil

1 small onion, finely chopped

1–2 garlic cloves, finely chopped

2 tsp ground turmeric

1 cinnamon stick

2 bay leaves

salt and black pepper

300ml (½ pint) chicken stock or water

200g (7oz) spinach, washed and thick stalks removed

1 Tip the rice into a bowl and cover with cold water. Leave to soak for 30 minutes, then rinse and drain. Heat the oil in a saucepan over a medium heat and cook the onion until soft and pale gold. Add the garlic and cook gently for 2 minutes, add the spices and bay leaves and turn them over in the oil for a couple of minutes more.

2 Stir in the rice, season and add the stock or water. Bring to the boil, then reduce the heat to very low and cover the pan. Cook for 15–20 minutes, or until the rice is tender and the stock has been absorbed. You may have to add a little more liquid but, if so, just pour in a little bit at a time. Do not stir the rice as it is cooking.

3 Put the spinach in a large saucepan with the water that is left clinging to the leaves after washing. Cover and set over a low heat. Cook for 4 minutes, or until wilted, turning the leaves over halfway through. Leave until cool enough to handle, then squeeze the excess water out. Chop roughly and season. When the rice is almost cooked, stir in the spinach and replace the lid for a couple of minutes to heat through. Fork through the rice to fluff it up before serving.

Sometimes you want a more colourful rice dish to dub up a plain piece of chicken or fish. Here's a really simple way to do this, using the Rasta colours of red, green and yellow, or as we say, gold. Use an empty coconut-milk can as a measure for your rice.

# Red, green and gold coconut rice

Serves 6

1 canful of long-grained rice (measure this using the empty coconut-milk can)

1 red pepper, deseeded and cut into 2cm (¾in) dice

1 green pepper, deseeded and cut into 2cm (¾in) dice

1 yellow pepper, deseeded and cut into 2cm (¾in) dice

400ml can coconut milk

few thyme sprigs

1 hot red chilli (ideally Scotch Bonnet), deseeded and finely chopped

salt and black pepper

1 Tip the rice into a bowl and cover with cold water. Leave to soak for 30 minutes, then rinse it really well and drain.

2 Put all the ingredients in a saucepan that has a tight-fitting lid and add 400ml (14fl oz) water. Stir to combine, cover and bring to the boil. Reduce the heat and simmer for 10–15 minutes, or until the rice has absorbed the liquid. Do not stir the rice while it is cooking or it will release starch.

3 Remove the pan from the heat and allow it to sit, covered, for another 10 minutes. Fork through the rice to fluff it up before serving, and season well.

Known as *arroz verde* in Spanish, this dish looks brilliant because of the bright colours. Try it with my Cuban Roast Pork (*see* page 111).

# Cuban green rice

Serves 6

340g (11¾oz) long-grain white rice

2 green peppers, deseeded and roughly chopped

2 spring onions, roughly chopped

50g (1¾oz) parsley, roughly chopped

25g (1oz) fresh coriander leaves, roughly chopped

salt, to taste

2 tbsp olive oil

25g (1oz) unsalted butter

475ml (17fl oz) chicken stock

juice of 1 lime

1 Tip the rice into a bowl and cover with cold water. Leave to soak for 30 minutes, then rinse it really well and drain.

2 Put the peppers, spring onions, parsley and coriander in a blender or food processor. Season with salt, add 2 tbsp water and whizz until smooth.

3 Place a saucepan that has a tight-fitting lid over a medium heat, pour in the oil and melt the butter. When the butter starts to foam, add the rice, stirring well to coat each grain, then mix in the herb paste. Cook for 1 minute, then stir in the stock. Bring to the boil, then reduce the heat to low. Cover and cook until the liquid has been completely absorbed and the rice is tender, about 16 minutes. Do not stir the rice while it is cooking or it will release starch.

4 Remove the pan from the heat and allow it to sit, covered, for 5 minutes. Uncover and squeeze over the lime juice. Fork through the rice to fluff it up before serving.

This is one of the essential dishes of Cuba, a staple in every home. The beans are seasoned up with what they call a *sofrito*, in this case a mixture of onion, garlic, cumin and oregano. It's certainly one of the most garlicky recipes I've done – on the whole I prefer this flavour nice and quiet – but they like it in Cuba and it certainly works well with black beans. Remember to soak the beans the night before you want to eat them. Serve with rice or just with a dollop of soured cream and some tortilla chips.

# Black beans, Cuban style

Serves 4–6

250g (9oz) black beans

½ green pepper, deseeded and left whole

2 bay leaves

1 tbsp sunflower oil

1 onion, roughly chopped

3 garlic cloves, finely chopped

½ tsp ground cumin

leaves from a large oregano sprig

splash of white wine vinegar

1 tsp caster sugar

salt and black pepper

1 Cover the beans with water and leave to soak overnight. The next day, drain and rinse them and place in a saucepan that has a lid with enough fresh water to cover. Add the green pepper and bay leaves. Bring to the boil, then reduce the heat, cover and simmer for 45 minutes, or until the beans are tender.

2 Meanwhile, to make the *sofrito*, pour the oil into a frying pan over a medium heat and add the onion and garlic. Cook, stirring occasionally, for about 5 minutes to soften a little. Add the cumin and oregano. Season with the vinegar and sugar to taste, cooking for another 1–2 minutes to combine the flavours. Season to taste.

3 Drain the cooked beans and remove the bay leaves and green pepper. Mash the beans slightly to make a soft, thick and textured dish. Stir in the *sofrito* and serve.

Parties

These delicious little Cuban snacks are great with a rum cocktail or a beer. The Cubans like them savoury, but those with a sweet tooth may like to dust them with sugar instead of salt. Dip your teaspoon in cold water before you put it in the sweetcorn batter, to help the mixture slip off easily into the hot oil.

# Sweetcorn fritoritos

Serves 6

2 boiled cobs sweetcorn or 1 × 200g can sweetcorn, drained

1 egg

2 tbsp fresh coriander leaves

pinch of salt, plus extra to serve (optional)

2–4 tbsp plain flour

½ tbsp double cream, if needed

sunflower oil, for deep-frying

To serve

juice of 1 lime

demerara sugar (optional)

1 If using corn cobs, cut the corn from the cobs by standing each cob on its stalk end and running a large knife down the sides. Put the corn – boiled or canned – in a blender or food processor with the egg, coriander and a pinch of salt. Add 2 tbsp of the flour. Whizz briefly to get a paste, adding the cream or more flour if necessary. You want a stiff paste that will form easily into balls.

2 Pour enough oil into a medium saucepan to come halfway up the sides, then place it over a medium heat until the temperature on a cook's thermometer is 190°C/375°F, or until a little nugget of the fritorito batter goes pale gold in about 45 seconds when dropped into the oil.

3 Gently drop teaspoonfuls of the paste into the hot oil, 4–5 at a time, and fry, turning over once or twice, until the fritoritos are golden brown on the outside and cooked within. Do not overcrowd the pan; you'll have to do these in batches. Drain on kitchen paper to remove any excess oil, and keep warm while you finish the rest. To serve, squeeze over a little lime juice and dust either with sugar or extra salt.

Jamaicans have nice thick water biscuits that are used both as biscuits and in cooking, but you could use any kind for this cracker-snack. It's a little treat, a pick-me-up that you can serve with a drink or just when you feel hungry. 'Cutters' are little round sandwiches eaten in the Caribbean and this is my quick and easy version.

# Mango and cream cheese 'cutters'

Serves 6 as a snack

¼ ripe mango, peeled

100g (3½oz) cream cheese

4 tsp chopped fresh coriander leaves

12 thick water biscuits or crackers

12 fresh coriander leaves, to garnish

1 Slice the mango flesh into thin strips.

2 Mix the cream cheese with the chopped coriander in a bowl. Spread the crackers with the cream cheese mixture. Top with strips of mango and garnish each 'cutter' with a fresh coriander leaf.

I like the surprise of the mint in this fresh, healthy dish. It's really important to slice the onion and coriander finely.

# Ceviche, Cuban style

Serves 4

250g (9oz) very fresh skinless salmon fillet, cut into 1cm (½in) dice

½ small red onion, very finely sliced

2 tbsp fresh coriander leaves, finely chopped

tortilla chips, to serve (optional)

For the dressing

50ml (2fl oz) lime juice

1 tbsp sunflower oil

6 mint leaves, roughly chopped

1 bay leaf

pinch of salt

1 Mix together all the ingredients for the dressing in a shallow non-reactive dish. Add the salmon and stir to ensure the fish is well coated. Cover with clingfilm and leave in the refrigerator for 2–3 hours, stirring a couple of times as the salmon marinates.

2 Stir in the onion and fresh coriander and serve the ceviche on its own or with a handful of tortilla chips on each plate.

Try this hot and sweet one-hit sauce! It's delicious with chicken, prawns, lamb – or just a pile of crisps.

# Pineapple, apricot and chilli dipper

Makes 500ml (18fl oz)

1 hot red chilli (ideally Scotch Bonnet), seeds left in or removed, depending on how hot you like it, finely chopped

400g (14oz) fresh pineapple, cut into 3cm (1¼in) chunks

3 large apricots, destoned and cut into 3cm (1¼in) chunks

2 tbsp tomato purée

1–2 tbsp cider vinegar, to taste

3–4 tbsp light brown muscovado sugar, to taste

good grating of nutmeg

½ garlic clove, finely chopped

1½ tsp salt

1 Put all the ingredients in a blender or food processor and whizz up to get a thick, smooth sauce. Taste, and add more sugar or vinegar if necessary.

2 Pour the sauce into a small bowl, cover with clingfilm and keep in the refrigerator until needed. Eat within a few days to enjoy this big dipper at its best.

This is a strange one! Eaten as a kind of pre-meal tongue-tickler, it is basically lightly pickled mango. It's irresistible once you've tried it and great in hot weather with a long, cool drink.

# Souscaille

Serves 4 as an appetiser

1 large mango, slightly under-ripe, peeled and stoned (*see* page 25)

2 garlic cloves, crushed

½ tsp salt

½ tsp white pepper

1 red chilli, deseeded and finely chopped

juice of 2 limes

1 Slice the mango cheeks into neat pieces, then carefully remove the mango flesh from the sides of the stone and cut into nice slices.

2 Mix all the other ingredients together with 200ml (7fl oz) water in a bowl. Add the mango slices to this marinade and leave for 20 minutes. Lift the mango slices out and serve. They will taste slightly pickled, hot and delicious.

These are so good with a glass of beer or a refreshing lime wash, or even sprinkled over ice cream. Irresistible!

# Sweet toasted coconut

Serves 6

6 tsp demerara sugar

175g (6oz) fresh coconut
(about 1 coconut)

1 Preheat the oven to 110°C/225°F/gas mark ¼. Line a baking sheet with foil. Mix the sugar with 6 tbsp hot water in a bowl, stirring to dissolve the sugar.

2 Use a vegetable peeler to slice long, thin slithers of coconut, ideally 5–6cm (2–2½in) long. Mix with the demerara syrup and spread the coconut pieces on the baking sheet. They don't need to be in one single layer, but try to give them as much space as possible.

3 Cook for 1 hour 10 minutes, or until lightly browned and crispy-dry. Store in an airtight container until needed – they will keep for a few days, but they won't last for long, I promise!

Wow...this is a pure chocolate hit! Chilli and chocolate is a great combination and chocolate makers large and small now make chilli-spiked chocolate bars. What you want in these smooth, rich truffles, based on a recipe by the chef Shaun Hill, is a really strong chocolate taste followed by a beautiful chilli buzz.

# Chocolate, chilli and rum truffles

Makes about 30

150g (5½oz) chilli chocolate

80ml (2½fl oz) double cream

75g (2¾oz) butter, softened

3 tsp rum

For the coating

100g (3½oz) chilli chocolate

3 tbsp cocoa powder

1 Melt the chocolate in a bowl suspended over a pan of simmering water (make sure the base of the bowl doesn't touch the water). Meanwhile, heat the cream in a saucepan until it's just boiling. Cool slightly, then pour into the melted chocolate and stir together. Whisk the butter until it becomes light and fluffy, then whisk in the chocolate cream followed by the rum. Leave to cool, then put in the refrigerator for 1–2 hours, or until firm enough to handle.

2 Melt the chocolate for the truffle coating in the same way as before. Leave to cool slightly. Scoop out large teaspoonfuls of the chilled chocolate mixture and shape into balls or ovals, or more rough-and-ready shapes, as you like. You can do the shaping with your hands – a messy but delightful business – or more neatly with 2 teaspoons.

3 Roll each truffle in the melted chocolate, then place on a tray covered in greaseproof paper until the coating has nearly set. (If the truffles are a little soft when you coat them in the melted chocolate, firm them up for 15 minutes in the freezer or 30 minutes in the refrigerator before continuing.) Dust each truffle with sifted cocoa powder and keep in the refrigerator – they last for a week or so, but you'll eat them well before this! Serve in *petit four* cake cases, if liked.

Oh, I know Pimm's is as English as strawberries and cream, but it can still be given the Caribbean treatment. Pimm's with a kick! Try to get the tasty Sicilian variety of lemonade, if you can. Just make sure none of your guests are driving!

# Dubbed-up Pimm's

Serves 6

250ml (9fl oz) Pimm's

600ml (1 pint) really good-quality lemonade

50ml (2fl oz) Curaçao

50ml (2fl oz) good rum

juice of 1 lime

To serve

lime slices

mango chunks

mint leaves

1 Mix everything together in a jug and add plenty of ice.

2 Serve with the lime slices, mango chunks and mint leaves.

This recipe was a long time in development. I wanted to get the balance of coffee to rum exactly right (a terrible job!) It might seem like very strong coffee but – believe me – it works. Chill really well, get into your hammock and enjoy!

# Iced rum coffee

Serves 6

9 tbsp ground coffee

2 tbsp sugar

1 cinnamon stick, broken in half

generous grating of nutmeg

100ml (3½fl oz) dark rum

5 tbsp whipping cream

6 tbsp condensed milk

1 Make the coffee with 700ml (1¼ pints) boiling water, stir in the sugar and spices and leave to cool completely.

2 Add all the other ingredients and chill well in the refrigerator.

3 Pour over ice in tall glasses to serve.

This punch is very simple and very delicious. Don't be tempted to add lime – it doesn't need it. The passion fruit pulp provides enough acidity on its own.

# Passion fruit, mango and orange punch

Serves 6

12 passion fruit

300ml (½ pint) freshly squeezed orange juice

300ml (½ pint) mango juice

6 tbsp caster sugar

150ml (5fl oz) rum

4 tbsp Curaçao

To serve

ice cubes

mango slices

orange wedges

1 Scoop the pulp and juice out of the passion fruit and strain to remove the seeds. Mix the juice with the orange and mango juices, sugar, rum and Curaçao.

2 Add ice and stir really well. Serve with slices of fresh mango and orange wedges.

This is the pure taste of the Caribbean. Rum, lime and sugar –
what could be better?

# Iced daiquiri

Serves 1

85ml (3fl oz) white rum

2½ tbsp lime juice, plus extra
for the glass

2 tsp caster sugar, plus extra
for the glass

generous handful of crushed ice

curl of lime zest, to decorate

1 Put the rum, lime juice, sugar and ice in a blender or food
processor and whizz until you have a mixture that looks like snow.

2 Squeeze some lime juice on to a small saucer. Pour some caster
sugar on to a second small saucer. Carefully stand a Champagne
coupe upside down in the lime juice, then in the caster sugar, to
coat the rim of the glass.

3 Pour the daiquiri into the glass and decorate with a curl of lime zest.

Pudding

I love this pannacotta, which is subtle as well as having the characteristic dub-it-up flavours of nutmeg, vanilla and honey. You will need four 125ml (4fl oz) ramekins or individual metal pudding moulds.

# Vanilla, nutmeg and honey pannacotta

Serves 4

250ml (9fl oz) double cream

200ml (7fl oz) whole milk

good grating of nutmeg

4 tsp gently flavoured honey (orange blossom, acacia or English wildflower)

1 vanilla pod

5 gelatine sheets

strawberry halves, to decorate

1 Put the cream, milk, nutmeg and honey in a small saucepan. Cut the vanilla pod in half. Scrape the seeds into the creamy mixture and also add the pod. Gently heat, stirring, for a couple of minutes, or until the liquid is just coming up to the boil. Remove from the heat and leave to infuse for 30 minutes, covered.

2 Soak the gelatine sheets in cold water for 5 minutes. Meanwhile, gently reheat the cream mixture. Take out the vanilla pod (wash and dry it for using another time, or put it in a bag of sugar to make vanilla sugar). Squeeze the water out of the gelatine and stir it into the scented cream mixture over a low heat until it has dissolved.

3 Pour the mixture into the ramekins or pudding moulds, cover with clingfilm and leave to set in the refrigerator for 2 hours, but not too much longer – you want to keep the texture nice and tender.

4 Loosen the pannacottas by slipping a knife gently around the edges. Dip the moulds briefly in hot water, then invert each on to a serving plate. The tops will be speckled with vanilla seeds and nutmeg. Decorate them with strawberry halves, then serve.

Muscovado sugar has a beautiful rich flavour and turns a regular meringue into a creamy Caribbean treat.

# Muscovado meringues

Makes 16

2 egg whites

50g (1¾oz) caster sugar

50g (1¾oz) light muscovado sugar

150ml (5fl oz) double cream,
to serve

1 Preheat the oven to 110°C/225°F/gas mark ¼. In a clean bowl, beat the egg whites until stiff. Gradually add the sugars, a little at a time, continuing to beat until the mixture has a smooth, shiny, thick consistency.

2 Line 2 baking sheets with greaseproof paper. Spoon on the meringue in small mounds, leaving a little space between them. Place in the oven for 1½ hours, or until the meringues feel dry to the touch. Cool in the oven with the door slightly open.

3 Store the meringues in an airtight container for up to a couple of days. When ready to serve, whisk the double cream until stiff and use it to sandwich pairs of the meringues together.

Is this good, or is this good? It includes some of my favourite ingredients, lovely dark chocolate, zesty orange, rum and cream!

# Chocolate, rum and raisin mousse

Serves 6

2 tbsp raisins

4 tsp rum

1½ tsp finely grated unwaxed orange zest

100g (3½oz) dark chocolate

4 large eggs, separated

3–4 tbsp caster sugar

single cream, to serve

1 Put the raisins and rum in a small saucepan. Warm over a gentle heat for a couple of minutes, then remove from the heat and stir in the orange zest. Leave the raisins to soak in the rum for 30 minutes.

2 Melt the chocolate in a bowl suspended over a pan of simmering water (make sure the base of the bowl doesn't touch the water), then leave to cool a little; don't skip this step, or you'll make chocolate scrambled eggs instead of mousse! Stir the cooled, melted chocolate into the egg yolks. Stir in the soaked raisins and some sugar, adding more or less depending on how much of a sweet tooth you have.

3 In a clean bowl, whisk the egg whites until they form stiff peaks. To help keep as much air in the soufflé as possible when folding the whisked egg whites into the chocolate mixture, first stir in just 1–2 spoonfuls to loosen it up, then continue with the rest of the egg white, which should then fold in more easily.

4 Pour the mousse into a soufflé dish or individual serving dishes. Chill for at least 4 hours, or overnight. Serve with single cream poured over the top.

Serves 4

Think this doesn't sound good? It's fabulocious! Based on one of my favourite Caribbean drinks, Caribbean stout punch, this is sweet and bitter, and brilliant with chocolate sauce or chocolate brownies. Serve it with a spoonful or two of rum poured over.

# Spiced stout ice cream

Serves 8

| | |
|---|---|
| 250ml (9fl oz) milk | 1 tsp vanilla extract |
| 250ml (9fl oz) double cream | 6 egg yolks |
| ½ cinnamon stick | 60g (2¼oz) soft dark brown sugar |
| 4 cloves | 150ml (5fl oz) stout |
| generous grating of fresh nutmeg | 2 tbsp dark rum |

1 Put the milk, cream, cinnamon and cloves in a saucepan and bring slowly to the boil. Take the pan off the heat, stir in the nutmeg and vanilla extract and leave to cool for 20 minutes. Remove and discard the cinnamon and cloves.

2 Meanwhile, beat the egg yolks with the sugar until fluffy. Add the cream mixture to the eggs and sugar, stirring constantly, then transfer to a heavy-based pan set over a very low heat. Cook gently, stirring with a wooden spoon, until the mixture is thick enough to coat the back of it. When done, pour into a bowl set in a sink of cold water to prevent further cooking. Stir in the stout and rum. Leave to cool.

3 Churn the ice cream according to the instructions on your ice cream maker, if you have one, or pour into a broad, shallow container and place in the freezer for 45 minutes, or until it is beginning to freeze around the edges. With the latter method you have to take the ice cream out and whip it up until smooth and creamy, either by tipping it into a blender or food processor and whizzing, or by churning it up with a fork and some elbow grease. Repeat this process twice more, then return to the freezer until ready to serve.

This has an amazingly intense banana flavour. And the good news is you don't need an ice cream maker for this recipe.

# Roast banana ice cream

Serves 6

4 bananas

8 tbsp soft light brown sugar

2 tbsp white rum

juice of 4 limes

250ml (9fl oz) whipping cream

200ml (7fl oz) full-fat milk

1 Preheat the oven to 180°C/350°F/gas mark 4. Peel the bananas, then halve them and put them in a small ovenproof dish. Sprinkle over the sugar, rum and the juice of 2 limes. Bake until completely tender; how long this takes depends on the ripeness of the bananas, but it shouldn't take longer than 15 minutes.

2 In a blender or food processor, whizz the bananas with the rest of the lime juice, then leave to cool. Whip the cream until it holds its shape. Mix the milk into the banana mixture, then add the cream and stir until there are no lumps left. Pour into a shallow container, cover and freeze. The brilliant thing about this recipe is that it doesn't require any churning or stirring.

Try to find a deep red watermelon as it will give your granita
a truly sensational colour.

# Watermelon and mint granita

Serves 8

1.5kg (3lb 5oz) watermelon,
deseeded and cubed

80g (3oz) caster sugar

generous handful of mint leaves,
roughly torn

finely grated zest and juice
of 3 limes

5 tbsp white rum

watermelon slices, to serve
(optional)

1 Toss the watermelon in a bowl with the sugar and mint and
allow to sit for an hour. Purée in a blender or food processor, then
add the lime juice. Push the mixture through a sieve into a shallow
container. Add the zest and rum and transfer to the freezer.

2 Roughly break up the crystals about 3 times during the freezing
process; you just need to use a fork to mash the granita.

3 Fork well again just before serving in well-chilled glasses with
slices of watermelon, if you like.

I love sweet, over-the-top desserts, but sometimes it's good to have something uncomplicated and clean. This is great after an exotic meal as it is quite simple. Add more rum if you want.

# Mangos in ginger and rum syrup

Serves 6–8

juice of 4 limes

400g (14oz) caster sugar

3cm (1¼in) fresh root ginger, peeled and cut into rounds

4 tbsp white rum

3 mangos, peeled, stoned and neatly sliced (*see* page 25)

2 pieces of preserved stem ginger in syrup, finely sliced into matchsticks

zest of 2 unwaxed limes, finely grated

1 Heat the lime juice, sugar and ginger together with 600ml (1 pint) water in a saucepan over a medium heat, stirring from time to time to help the sugar dissolve. Bring to the boil, then reduce the heat and simmer for about 25 minutes, until the mixture is syrupy. It will thicken more as it cools. Add the rum. Leave to cool, then strain to remove the ginger.

2 Put the mango slices in a bowl and pour over the syrup. Chill well. Scatter with the preserved ginger and lime zest and serve.

This dish looks like a big Easter bonnet of a pudding. You can add to the fruit, using bananas (make sure you squeeze lemon juice over them so they don't go brown) or orange segments – whatever takes your fancy.

# Coconut pavlova with tropical fruit

Serves 8

6 egg whites, at room temperature

pinch of salt

375g (13oz) caster sugar

2 tsp cornflour

1 tsp white wine vinegar

4 tbsp desiccated coconut

600ml (1 pint) double cream

4 tbsp white rum

icing sugar, to taste

For the topping

1 papaya, peeled, deseeded and sliced

2 small mangos, peeled, stoned and neatly sliced (*see* page 25)

1 baby pineapple, peeled and chopped

6 passion fruit, halved, juice and seeds scooped out

1 Preheat the oven to 180°C/350°F/gas mark 4. Put the egg whites in a large, clean bowl with the salt and beat with an electric whisk. When the mixture forms medium-sized peaks, add the sugar 1 tbsp at a time, whisking after each addition, then whisk in the cornflour, vinegar and coconut until you have a very stiff, glossy mixture.

2 Line 2 baking sheets with greaseproof paper and spread the meringue out to make 2 × 20cm (8in) rounds. Put in the oven for 5 minutes, then turn the heat down to 130°C/270°F/gas mark ¾ and cook for about an hour, until lightly toasted and crisp on the outside, but soft and marshmallowy in the centre. Leave to cool. Whip the cream until it holds its shape, then whisk in the rum and icing sugar.

3 Put a meringue disc on a serving platter (a tall cake stand looks good). Top with half the cream and half the fruit (but reserve the passion fruit). Place the other meringue on top, then finish with another layer of cream, and the rest of the fruit, ending with the passion fruit pulp drizzled over the top.

This baked cheesecake is so delicious, sweetened with butterscotchy muscovado sugar and flavoured with ginger, lime and vanilla.

# Ginger and muscovado cheesecake

Serves 8–10

175g (6oz) gingernuts

75g (2¾oz) butter, plus extra for the tin

For the filling

500g (1lb 2oz) full-fat cream cheese

4 eggs, separated

200g (7oz) light brown muscovado sugar

1 tsp vanilla extract

zest of 2 limes, finely grated

5 pieces of preserved stem ginger in syrup, finely chopped

300ml (½ pint) soured cream

25–50g (1–1¾oz) pecans, to decorate

1 Preheat the oven to 200°C/400°F/gas mark 6. Put the gingernuts in a food processor and whizz to turn them into crumbs. Transfer to a bowl. Melt the butter and mix with the biscuit crumbs. Press the buttered crumbs into the bottom of a 20cm (8in) diameter springform cake tin in an even layer, and push them about 4cm (1½in) up the sides. Put in the oven and bake for 10 minutes.

2 Take the base out of the oven and leave to cool slightly, then lightly grease the sides of the tin above the biscuit mixture. Reduce the oven temperature to 160°C/325°F/gas mark 3.

3 Mix the cream cheese with the egg yolks, then stir in the sugar, vanilla, lime zest and preserved ginger. Whisk the egg whites until stiff, then carefully fold into the cheesecake mixture. Pour into the tin on top of the gingernut base. Place the tin on a baking sheet, and cook for 1 hour, or until almost set. Leave, with the oven turned off and the door closed, for another 30 minutes, then remove from the oven and allow to cool completely.

4 Whisk the soured cream until thick and spread it over the top of the cheesecake. Decorate with pecans. Keep the cheesecake in the refrigerator until ready to serve.

*Blancmange my style is far from bland. This is a sweet and shining coconut tower, served with some golden mangos.*

# Coconut blancmange with mango

Serves 8

11 gelatine sheets

450ml can coconut milk

405g can condensed milk

3 ripe mangos

finely grated zest and juice of 1 lime

1 Cover the gelatine with cold water and leave to soak for 5 minutes. Meanwhile, put the coconut milk and the condensed milk in a saucepan. Warm gently, stirring to combine. Make sure it is not too hot and keep stirring, or it will catch on the bottom of the pan.

2 Drain and gently squeeze the gelatine to get rid of the excess water and stir it into the coconut mixture, over a low heat, until it completely dissolves. Pour this into a 1 litre (1¾ pint) jelly mould or pudding basin. Leave to cool, then put in the refrigerator to set. It should be ready in a couple of hours.

3 Cut both 'cheeks' from the mango stones and cross-hatch the flesh into roughly 2cm (¾in) cubes, making sure your knife goes right down to the skin but not through it. Press the centre of each piece of mango skin with your fingers so that the straight, cut flesh side becomes rounded (it will look like a mango hedgehog). You could leave the mango like this, or use the knife to cut off the cubes of flesh. Remove the rest of the flesh from the stones, peel and cut into cubes about the same size. However you cut it, put the mango in a bowl and squeeze over the lime juice.

4 To unmould the blancmange, gently slip a knife around the edge, then dip the mould in a bowl of hot water for 10 seconds. Put a wet serving plate on top and invert the blancmange on to the centre of the plate. (The wet plate helps to slide the blancmange around if it comes out off-centre.) Place the mango 'hedgehogs' on the side or pile the mango around the gleaming white coconut blancmange, and serve sprinkled with grated lime zest.

Forget tinned fruit and bottles of sherry, this is the best trifle you will ever taste. Use a good tub of fresh custard to make it.

# Mango, passion fruit and banana trifle

Serves 6

2 mangos, peeled and stoned (*see* page 25)

5 passion fruit

1 banana

300g (10½oz) bought sponge cake

4 tbsp lemon curd

50ml (2fl oz) rum

juice of 1 lime

500g tub custard

250ml (9fl oz) whipping cream

icing sugar, to taste

toasted coconut flakes, toasted flaked almonds or more passion fruit pulp and seeds, to decorate

1 Cut the mango flesh into cubes or slices – whichever you prefer. Halve the passion fruit and scoop out the pulp and seeds. Slice the banana neatly.

2 Now you just have to assemble the trifle. Cut the sponge into wide fingers and spread each one with lemon curd. Put a double layer of these curd side up in the bottom of a glass bowl. Sprinkle with half the rum, then add a layer of the fruits. Squeeze half the lime on the fruit, then add half the custard. Repeat the layers one more time, making sure you use everything up. You need to finish with a layer of custard. Cover with clingfilm and put in the refrigerator. It will taste much better the next day.

3 Whip the cream into medium peaks and add enough icing sugar to satisfy your sweet tooth. Spread this on top of the trifle and decorate with coconut, almonds or passion fruit, as you prefer.

A beautiful, golden pudding, this is a Jamaican classic. Back in the Caribbean, we often make it in a pot over hot coals with more piled on a lid on top. As the saying goes, 'Hell-ah-top, Hell-ah-bottom – and Hallelujah in the middle!'

# Sweet potato pudding

Serves 10–12

100g (3½oz) raisins

juice of 1 orange

1 tbsp rum

100g (3½oz) butter, melted, plus extra for the tin

1kg (2lb 4oz) sweet potato, grated

200g (7oz) soft brown sugar

200g (7oz) plain flour

3 tsp ground cinnamon

1 tsp grated nutmeg

1 tsp salt

3 tsp vanilla extract

200ml (7fl oz) coconut milk

2 large eggs

single cream, to serve

1 Preheat the oven to 180°C/350°F/gas mark 4. Put the raisins in a small saucepan with the orange juice and rum. Bring to the boil, turn off the heat and leave to soak for 10 minutes or while you prepare the other ingredients.

2 Grease a 26cm (10½in) springform cake tin with butter. Put the potato in a big mixing bowl with the sugar, flour, cinnamon, nutmeg and salt. Mix well with your hands so the potato is coated in sugar and spices. In another, smaller bowl, mix together the vanilla extract, coconut milk, melted butter and eggs, then add in the raisins and any of their liquid. Stir this into the sweet potato mixture.

3 Pour the batter into the cake tin and cook in the hot oven for 1¼–1½ hours, or until firm. This is a pudding rather than a cake and is meant to be moist inside. Eat hot, warm or cold – and definitely with cream. I love cream, and in this case it is essential.

High Tea

This is a chocolate cake with knobs on: the orange zest and spices give it a Caribbean twist. It's brilliant after a luxurious supper with some cream on the side and strong cups of coffee, or served in the afternoon with an icy cold glass of milk.

# Chocolate and orange spice cake

Serves 8

175g (6oz) blanched almonds

4 large eggs, separated

170g (5¾oz) caster sugar

75g (2¾oz) plain chocolate, grated

zest of 2 unwaxed oranges, finely grated

1 tbsp ground cinnamon

2 tbsp orange juice

butter, for the tin

candied orange peel, to decorate

For the chocolate cream

140g (5oz) plain chocolate, broken into pieces

150ml (5fl oz) soured cream

½ tbsp caster sugar

1 Toast the almonds in a dry frying pan over a low heat. Watch them all the time as they go from pale to burnt very quickly. Tip into a bowl to cool, then grind them in a food processor. Preheat the oven to 180°C/350°F/gas mark 4.

2 Beat the egg yolks with half the sugar, using an electric mixer or by hand, until pale and fluffy. In a separate clean bowl, beat the egg whites, gradually adding the remaining sugar, until soft peaks form.

3 Stir the almonds, chocolate, orange zest, cinnamon and orange juice into the beaten egg yolks. Mix well. Using a large metal spoon, add a third of the egg whites to the chocolate mixture and gently fold in, then fold in the rest. Pour into a buttered and base-lined 20cm (8in) tin and bake for 35–40 minutes, or until a skewer inserted into the centre comes out clean. Turn out on to a wire rack and leave to cool.

4 To make the chocolate cream, put the chocolate in a bowl set over a pan of simmering water (make sure the base of the bowl isn't touching the water). Add the soured cream and sugar and melt everything together. Stir well to combine. Take off the heat and leave to cool and thicken. Spread over the top of the cake with a palette knife and sprinkle over the candied orange peel.

I am a big fan of lemon drizzle cake, but I wanted to make a more Caribbean version, so I've tried it with limes – and it's even better! Make this once and it will become part of your repertoire.

# Lime drizzle cake

Serves 8

125g (4½oz) butter, diced, plus extra for the tin

225g (8oz) self-raising flour, sifted

pinch of salt

125g (4½oz) caster sugar

2 large eggs, beaten

finely grated zest and juice of 3 unwaxed limes

For the topping

juice of 2 limes

100g (3½oz) caster sugar

icing sugar, to dust (optional)

1 Preheat the oven to 180°C/350°F/gas mark 4. Butter a 900g (2lb) loaf tin and line with greaseproof paper.

2 Mix the flour and salt together in a large bowl, then rub in the butter until the mixture resembles breadcrumbs. Stir in the sugar. Add the eggs and the lime zest and juice and mix together.

3 Spoon the cake batter into the loaf tin and bake for 45–55 minutes, or until the cake is golden and well risen and a skewer inserted into the centre comes out clean. Leave to cool for 10 minutes, then lift the cake out of the tin.

4 Meanwhile, mix the lime juice and sugar for the topping together. Prick the cake surface all over with a skewer or fork, then pour the topping over and leave it to sink in. A sugary crust will form on top, which tastes delicious. Finish with a light dusting of icing sugar just before serving, if liked.

Serves 8

115g (4oz) butter, softened, plus extra for the tin

140g (5oz) soft light brown sugar

2 tsp vanilla extract

2 eggs, lightly beaten

zest of 1 unwaxed orange, finely grated

½ tsp ground cinnamon

3 ripe bananas, mashed

4 tbsp soured cream

225g (8oz) plain flour, sifted

1 tsp baking powder

½ tsp bicarbonate of soda

35g (1¼oz) chocolate chips

25g (1oz) pecans, roughly chopped

dried banana chips or roughly chopped pecans, to decorate

For the buttercream

170g (5¾oz) unsalted butter, slightly softened

340g (11¾oz) soft light brown sugar

juice of 1 lime

What is better than banana cake? Banana cake with chocolate! This is fabulously moist – do use very ripe bananas – and moreish. If you don't want the buttercream, just dust the top with icing sugar.

# Banana and chocolate chip cake

1 Preheat the oven to 180°C/350°F/gas mark 4. Butter a 20 × 13cm (8 × 5in) loaf tin and base-line with greaseproof paper.

2 Beat the butter and sugar together, using an electric mixer or by hand, until pale and fluffy. Add the vanilla extract, then the eggs, a little at a time, beating after each addition. The mixture should be smooth and creamy. Stir in the orange zest, cinnamon, bananas and soured cream, then fold in the flour, baking powder, bicarbonate of soda, chocolate chips and pecans.

3 Pour the batter into the loaf tin, transfer to the oven and bake for 1 hour, or until a skewer inserted into the centre of the cake comes out clean. Carefully turn out on to a wire rack and leave to cool.

4 For the buttercream, beat the butter and sugar together, using an electric mixer or by hand, until pale and fluffy. Stir in the lime juice. Put the buttercream in the refrigerator to firm up a little so that you can spread it easily – 20 minutes should do it. Don't leave it too long or it will become too hard.

5 When the cake is completely cold, spread over the buttercream. Decorate with dried banana chips or more chopped pecans.

Wow – this is definitely one for coffee- and rum-lovers. Make the coffee as strong as you can and don't be scared by the amount of liquid you are pouring into the cake. It soaks it up to make the most fabulocious boozy cake.

# Coffee rum cake

Serves 8

175g (6oz) butter, softened, plus extra for the tin

175g (6oz) soft light brown sugar

3 eggs, lightly beaten

175g (6oz) self-raising flour, sifted

pinch of salt

5 tbsp caster sugar

80ml (2½fl oz) rum

425ml (¾ pint) very strong hot coffee

300ml (½ pint) whipping cream

pecans, to decorate

1 Preheat the oven to 190°C/375°F/gas mark 5.

2 Beat the butter and brown sugar together, using an electric mixer or by hand, until pale and fluffy. Add the eggs a little at a time, beating well after each addition, then fold in the flour and salt. Put in a greased and base-lined ring mould, or 20cm (8in) cake tin, and bake for 30–40 minutes, or until a skewer inserted into the centre of the cake comes out clean. Turn out on to a wire rack and leave to cool.

3 Add the caster sugar and rum to the coffee and taste – you may want more sugar or rum to taste. Don't drink too much of it! Put the cake back in its tin and pierce it all over with a skewer, then pour the coffee slowly through the holes, soaking the sponge, and leave overnight.

4 Whip the cream into soft peaks. Turn out the cake and decorate with the cream and pecans.

This is a cake to serve to someone you love, or – even better – a whole crowd of people you adore! My recipe for Passion Fruit and Lime Curd is on page 186. If you don't have time to make this, cheat and stir some passion fruit juice and seeds into bought lemon curd.

# Passion fruit cake

Serves 8

200g (7oz) butter, slightly softened, plus extra for the tin

200g (7oz) caster sugar

zest of 2 unwaxed limes, finely grated

3 eggs, lightly beaten

200g (7oz) self-raising flour, sifted

For the filling

125g (4½oz) mascarpone cheese

75g (2¾oz) fromage frais

250g (9oz) Passion Fruit and Lime Curd (*see* page 186)

icing sugar, to taste and for dusting

1 Preheat the oven to 180°C/350°F/gas mark 4. Butter a 23cm (9in) cake tin and base-line with greaseproof paper.

2 Beat the sugar, butter and lime zest together, using an electric mixer or by hand, until pale and fluffy. Add the eggs a little at a time, beating well after each addition. If the mixture starts to curdle, add 1 tbsp of the flour. Fold in the rest of the flour with a large metal spoon, then scrape the batter into the cake tin. Bake for 35 minutes, or until a skewer inserted into the centre comes out clean and the cake is slightly coming away from the sides of the tin. Turn out on to a wire rack and leave to cool.

3 Carefully cut the cake horizontally, using a serrated knife, to give 2 thin layers. Set the bottom half on a plate. Lightly mix the mascarpone with the fromage frais, most of the curd and a little icing sugar. Taste – you may want to add more curd or sugar. Spread this filling over the sponge, then swirl the rest of the curd round the edges where you will see it peeking out the sides.

4 Place on the top layer of cake and dust with icing sugar.

This is an ambrosial concoction – food for the gods! Use it to fill cakes (there's a recipe on page 184), for topping scones, or just for spreading on your toast (I've also been known to have a spoonful on vanilla ice cream). Make sure your butter is at room temperature before you start.

# Passion fruit and lime curd

Makes 340g (12oz)

2 eggs, lightly beaten

125ml (4fl oz) passion fruit pulp (about 4 fruits)

finely grated zest and juice of 1 lime

80g (3oz) caster sugar

60g (2¼oz) unsalted butter, diced and softened

1 Put the eggs, passion fruit, lime zest and juice and sugar in a bowl set over a pan of simmering water. Stir continuously with a wooden spoon for 12 minutes, until the mixture becomes thick.

2 Remove from the heat and whisk in the butter. Leave to cool. Eat immediately, or spoon into a sterilised jar while still hot and seal (*see* page 125 for sterilising instructions). The curd will keep in the refrigerator for up to a week.

In Jamaica, we like to eat 'bun and cheese', and it is especially associated with Easter. Our bun is dark and large. This is another version, sweet and spicy, that is based on a British hot-cross bun... but this time with tropical fruits! When I was growing up in Clarendon, Jamaica, we only had red-coloured cheese, so one of my favourite cheeses is still Red Leicester.

# Tropical mini-bun and cheese

Makes 12

500–600g (1lb 2oz–1lb 5oz) strong white flour

7g packet easy-blend yeast

½ tsp salt

50–100g (1¾–3½oz) caster sugar (optional)

½–¾ tbsp mixed spice

2 eggs, beaten

75g (2¾oz) butter, melted, plus extra for the bowl and baking sheet, and to serve

220ml (8fl oz) milk, warmed

60g (2¼oz) currants

100g (3½oz) ready-to-eat mixed dried tropical fruits, chopped small

milk, to glaze

Red Leicester cheese, to serve

1 Put 500g (1lb 2oz) of the flour in a large bowl (you may need to add more later), then mix in the yeast and salt. Add the sugar (or not, depending on how sweet a tooth you have), and more or less of the spice, according to your taste. In another bowl, mix together the eggs, butter and milk. Make a well in the centre of the dry ingredients and pour the liquid in. Work the liquid into the dough, first using a table knife and then your hands. Knead together on a lightly floured work surface for about 10 minutes, until the dough is elastic and smooth.

2 Put the dough in a lightly oiled bowl, cover and leave to rise in a warm place for 1½ hours, or until doubled in size. Meanwhile, preheat the oven to 200°C/400°F/gas mark 6 and lightly grease a baking sheet.

3 Knead the dough again on a lightly floured work surface, adding more flour if necessary to get a workable, not-too-sticky dough. Work in the currants and tropical fruits. Divide the dough into 12 pieces and shape into small round buns. Brush with milk, to glaze. Place the mini-buns on the greased baking sheet and bake for 20 minutes, then transfer to a wire rack to cool.

4 Split the buns in half, spread the halves with butter and put a slice of Red Leicester, or other cheese, on to each half, or sandwich 2 halves together with the cheese in the middle.

Makes about 24

425g (15oz) plain flour, sifted

1 tsp baking powder

1 tsp ground cinnamon

good pinch of salt

225g can pineapple chunks, drained

225g (8oz) butter, softened

350g (12oz) soft light brown sugar

2 tsp vanilla extract

3 eggs, beaten

2 small very ripe bananas, mashed

100g (3½oz) pecans

100g (3½oz) desiccated coconut

zest of 2 unwaxed limes,
finely grated

24 pecans, to decorate

For the buttercream

170g (5¾oz) unsalted butter,
slightly softened

340g (11¾oz) icing sugar

juice of 1 lime

I am not going to be left out of the cupcake craze! These are beautilicious; good to look at and even better to eat. The batter is based on a recipe for the classic hummingbird cake (an Aussie favourite), but it contains loads of good Caribbean ingredients.

# Caribbean cupcakes

1 Preheat the oven to 180°C/350°F/gas mark 4. Mix the flour, baking powder, cinnamon and salt together in a large bowl. Purée the pineapple chunks in a blender or food processor.

2 Beat the butter and sugar together, using an electric mixer or by hand, until pale and fluffy. Add the vanilla extract, then gradually beat in the eggs, mixing well after each addition. Stir in the puréed pineapple, bananas, pecans, coconut and zest, then gradually fold in the flour. Divide between paper cake cases set in 2 × 12-cup cake trays, filling each case about two-thirds full. Bake for 12–15 minutes. The cupcakes are ready when they spring back to the touch or a skewer inserted into the centre comes out clean. Remove to a wire rack and leave to cool.

3 For the buttercream, beat the butter, icing sugar and lime juice together, using an electric mixer or by hand, until pale and fluffy. With a small palette knife, or blunt knife, spread the buttercream over the top of the cakes. Decorate each cake with a pecan.

Here's a delicious dubbed-up version of Scottish shortbread. These are perfect with a cup of tea or coffee, or scoops of vanilla ice cream.

# Pecan and ginger shortbread

Makes 16–20

125g (4½oz) unsalted butter, softened, plus extra for the tin

55g (2oz) caster sugar, plus ½ tbsp extra for sprinkling

150g (5½oz) plain flour, sifted

50g (1¾oz) fine cornmeal (polenta)

50g (1¾oz) pecans, chopped

1½ pieces of preserved stem ginger in syrup, finely chopped

1 Preheat the oven to 170°C/340°F/gas mark 3½.

2 Beat the butter and sugar together, using an electric mixer or by hand, until pale and fluffy, then stir in the flour and cornmeal (polenta) until smooth. Add the pecans and ginger and stir until they are evenly distributed.

3 Pack the shortbread into a liberally buttered 20cm (8in) square cake tin, using your fingertips to press it into a fairly even layer. Prick lightly all over with the prongs of a fork. Bake for around 30 minutes, or until the shortbread is pale brown, then remove from the oven and sprinkle with the extra sugar.

4 Leave the shortbread to cool in the tin, then cut into 16–20 squares.

You can use this recipe to make ginger biscuits as well, but there isn't a child who can resist a gingerbread man. If you feel like it, you can go mad on the decoration, using tubes of ready-made icing to make stripy jumpers in Caribbean colours or licorice shoelaces to give your gingerbread men dreadlocks!

# Gingerbread men

Makes 10

110g (3¾oz) butter, cubed, plus extra for the baking sheet

340g (11¾oz) plain flour, plus extra to dust

2 tsp ground ginger

1 tsp bicarbonate of soda

170g (5¾oz) soft dark brown sugar

1 egg, beaten

4 tbsp golden syrup

handful of currants, to decorate

1 Preheat the oven to 190°C/375°F/gas mark 5 and lightly grease a baking sheet with butter. Sift the flour, ginger and bicarbonate of soda into a bowl. Rub in the butter with your fingers until the mixture resembles breadcrumbs, then mix in the sugar and egg.

2 Warm the syrup in a pan over a very gentle heat to make it runny, then stir enough of it into the mixture to make a soft dough – be careful not to add too much. Knead on a lightly floured work surface until smooth, then flour a wooden board and your rolling pin and roll the dough out until it is about 5mm (¼in) thick.

3 Take a gingerbread man cutter and stamp out your shapes, carefully easing each out of the cutter and placing it on to the baking sheet (a fish slice is useful for this). Using the currants, give each man 2 eyes and a mouth.

4 Bake for about 12 minutes, or until just coloured, then carefully transfer to a wire rack to cool.

Serves 8–10

450g (1lb) dried mixed fruit (sultanas, currants, raisins and tropical fruits, cut into small chunks)

200ml (7fl oz) cold tea

150ml (5fl oz) dark rum

25g (1oz) butter, melted, plus extra for the tin and to serve

250g (9oz) stoneground wholemeal flour

1 tsp bicarbonate of soda

⅛ tsp ground cloves

⅛ tsp ground ginger

¼ tsp ground cinnamon

really generous grating of nutmeg

175g (6oz) light soft brown sugar

1 egg, lightly beaten

Easy, easy, easy! Just soak the fruit, mix and bake. This is a great bread for afternoon tea.

# Rum tea bread

1 Put the fruit in a saucepan and add the tea and rum. Bring to just under the boil, reduce the heat and simmer for 5 minutes. Take off the heat, cover, and leave the fruit to plump up for 24 hours.

2 Preheat the oven to 170°C/345°F/gas mark 3½.

3 Butter and line a 24 × 13cm (9½ × 5in) loaf tin, 6cm (2½in) deep, with greaseproof paper. In a mixing bowl, stir the fruit and tea together with all the remaining ingredients and mix until well combined. Spoon the batter into the tin and even out the top. Bake in the oven for about 1½ hours, or until the bread feels firm and a skewer inserted into the centre comes out clean. If the top is becoming too dark before it's fully cooked, cover with foil.

4 Leave the bread in the tin for 10 minutes after removing it from the oven, then turn out and cool on a wire rack. You can eat it in slices just as it is, or spread with butter.

Good cooking is about loving the things you put in your pot. You just need a little bit of this and a little bit of that to make the magic that delights your guests, body and soul. If you want a head start, get together my Sunshine Kit. It's the box of flavours I carry around with me to add a bit of sunshine to food. The Kit has fresh root ginger, chillies (ideally Scotch Bonnet), allspice, thyme, nutmeg, bay leaves and black pepper.

# My Favourite Ingredients

## Allspice (Pimento)

This fragrant spice is so typical of my food. I love it. More commonly called pimento in the Caribbean, it's often part of the famous Jamaican jerk seasoning that we put on meat, fish and even vegetables. The spice is essentially the dried berries of a beautiful tree that grows all over Jamaica. Whole allspice berries are great to put in a soup or stew. You can also buy powdered allspice for baking and seasoned-up marinades.

## Bananas

I always have bananas at my place. Green bananas are good for savoury dishes, but most of all I like the sweet ones, whether for a refreshing smoothie (*see* page 25), baked and served with passion fruit (*see* page 75), mashed up in my Banana and Chocolate Chip Cake (*see* page 182), or slightly caramelised in my Roast Banana Ice Cream (*see* page 164). It's a real utility fruit. And then, of course, you can always use the skin to slip somebody up! Look out for Caribbean bananas in the shops – they are nice and sweet – and quite a few are Fairtrade these days.

## Bay Leaves

I like to put bay leaves in all sorts of dishes, from porridge to soups. It's good to see a bit of bay leaf bouncing around in a stew! I grew up using the dried leaves, but fresh green ones are really good and it's so easy to plant a bay tree at home in a garden, or in a pot on a balcony. Bay leaf goes well in all sorts of dishes and its fragrance is essential in bean recipes such as my Black Beans, Cuban Style (*see* page 133).

## Beans (and peas)

Now is it beans or peas? In Jamaica, what other people call beans we call peas, as in the classic dish 'rice and peas', which is made with kidney beans. Whatever the name, beans and peas are my friends. Kidney beans and chickpeas in particular are used a lot in what we call 'ital' food, the pure, unprocessed dishes favoured by Rastafarians. Healthy, nourishing, warming and good value, bean and pea recipes appear frequently in this book, including the Cuban staple, Black Beans (*see* page 133), Caribbean Tamarind Chickpeas (*see* page 82) and there's even a Jamaican take on the famous baked beans, done Levi style (*see* page 38).

## Black pepper

This is far more than just a standard seasoning to go alongside salt. Black pepper is essential in my Sunshine Kit and I use it to give an aromatic heat to dishes. Crush the whole peppercorns yourself in a pestle and mortar to get the best flavour, or grind them freshly into food. Black pepper and salt are the only accessories you need for fried fish, while a good sprinkling of black pepper over dishes at the end of cooking makes all the difference, such as in my Sweet Potato, Red Onion and Feta Sunshine Tart (*see* page 52).

## Chicken

I grew up with chickens on my grandparents' farm in Jamaica. In fact, I had a chicken as my first pet! They also had another purpose, as food. Not only did we gather the eggs from the hens, we also ate our chickens. My grandfather taught me how to kill them properly. You learn so many lessons about life and death when you live on a farm. As a result, I value chickens and nothing is wasted. The carcass of the bird is a favourite in Jamaica. When I was growing up, legs, breasts and thighs were always too expensive, so ghetto-ites would cook up what was left – what we call 'chicken back' – in all different styles, to make real 'poor people food'. Delicious! These days, I like to cook chicken on the bone to get the most flavour, as in my Inside-out Chicken Supper (*see* page 106) and Chicken, Pepper and Squash Curry (*see* page 90).

## Chocolate

I never ate chocolate as a boy, but as an adult, I'm a chocoholic! I love a cup of tea with a nice block of chocolate, I cannot resist a good chocolate cake, and as for brownies – well – fantastic! This book has some real treats for my fellow chocolate lovers, such as Chocolate, Rum and Raisin Mousse (*see* page 160), Chocolate and Orange Spice Cake (*see* page 178) and, of course, my Chocolate, Chilli and Rum Truffles (*see* page 146): a pure shot of choc. In cooking, darker chocolate will give you the most intense flavour, so use bars with at least 60 per cent cocoa solids to get the best results.

## Coconut

My cooking makes the best of the fabulocious coconut, one of my most trusted and versatile ingredients. If you are buying the nut whole, give it a quick shake to check it still has liquid inside; this shows it is fresh. Poke a knife through the three indentations on the top to discover which one is the true hole, then pierce it right the way through. Pour out the juice and drink it on ice – it's delicious and healthy! Then you smash open the coconut on a hard surface, or put it in a bag and bang it with a hammer and prize out the flesh with a small knife. I like to use fresh coconut in my Sweet Toasted Coconut (*see* page 144). If you want to make fresh coconut milk, grate the flesh, soak it in warm water and squeeze out the liquid. But you can also easily buy coconut milk in cans. The top of the liquid in the cans is creamier than the rest and you can buy this thicker form of coconut – coconut cream – on its own in sachets or tubs. You can also buy the dried-out flesh as desiccated coconut. I use the unsweetened sort in my Coconut King Prawns (*see* page 60) and Coconut Pavlova with Tropical Fruit (*see* page 168).

## Fish

Having grown up on a Caribbean island, I love to eat fish. As a boy, I enjoyed snapper and freshwater perch, which I'd catch with my best friend Carlie. These days I eat quite a bit of sea bass and sea bream, which are nice and chunky. Another favourite is tilapia. I first saw it farmed in Africa and it's now widely available. It is easy to cook and eat because the fish has nice meaty fillets without bones; I use them in my Golden Tilapia Fishcakes (*see* page 42). In other dishes I like to eat fish whole, with the head kept on. You get lots of tasty, juicy flesh if you cook fish on the bone. Whatever fish you use, season it up well, Jamaican style, using plenty of salt and black pepper inside and out. One very special feast of a fish dish in this book is My Baked Christmas Fish (*see* page 104).

## Garlic

'Bleugh!' is what I used to think about garlic, but it is an essential ingredient. I love kissing, but not with garlic breath! I cook with garlic all the time and have evolved a way to tame the beast, which you can adopt for the recipes in this book. If you put the cloves into a dish whole, or cut them into bigger pieces, you get a more subtle fragrance. If you cut garlic up too small, it can overpower the other flavours in a dish.

## Ginger

Fresh root ginger is another crucial ingredient in my Sunshine Kit. I use it for a detoxing tea and also add it to carrot juice with lime and honey. Look for nice firm pieces with unwrinkled skin. And I'm a big fan of preserved stem ginger in syrup. Try it in sweet dishes, such as my simple Mangos in Ginger and Rum Syrup (*see* page 166), and in savoury recipes, such as the dressing on the Roast Squash, Chilli and Spinach Salad with Peanut and Ginger Dressing (*see* page 40). The fragrant syrup itself is useful and delicious in cooking.

## Honey

Now you're talking! I love honey. In the Caribbean, you often find it stored in old rum bottles, taken straight off the comb and still bursting with the natural, unfiltered goodness of the nectar that bees have gathered from the flowers. Honeys vary according to what the bees have fed on, so try different kinds and taste their flavours in dishes such as Vanilla, Nutmeg and Honey Pannacotta (*see* page 156). My grandfather kept bees so we used to eat honey from the comb, pure and simple. I find it a healthy alternative to sugar and it can go into all types of drinks, as well as food, to keep them natural, such as my Tropical Fruit and Honey Shake (*see* page 25).

## Lime

Limes are found everywhere in the Caribbean; we use them more than lemons. As well as using them in food, try squeezing out the juice and mixing it with water and sugar to make what we call a 'lime wash'. The fruit is also used to wipe down surfaces to keep a place nice and fresh. If you see limes in a kitchen, it indicates a clean household. The lime takes its proper place at centre stage in this book. You should try my delicious Lime Drizzle Cake (*see* page 180) and Lime and Thyme Lamb Chops (*see* page 67).

## Mango

When I was a boy in Jamaica, every garden had a mango tree. People even graft them on to other trees, so an avocado tree may grow a branch of mangos! I love to eat a mango fresh. In Jamaica, we wait until they are really ripe, then cut a hole in one end. You suck out the juice and flesh and are left with just the empty pouch of the skin and the seed. I also love to cook with mangos, when it is best if they are ripe but still firm. To learn how to cut the mango flesh off the stone, *see* page 25. I've also got a great recipe for slightly less ripe fruit, Souscaille (*see* page 143). Dried mango is another excellent ingredient, good for snacks and in the storecupboard for cooking.

## Nutmeg

For me, this is the number-one Caribbean spice. It suits both sweet and savoury dishes, such as creamy puddings and jerk spice mixtures. People say that nutmeg is an aphrodisiac...but they say that about most foods! Buy nutmeg whole and grate it fresh to get the most flavour. When I was a boy, I used to make the graters myself out of empty cans. I'd cut off the top and bottom and open up the side, then I'd use a nail to puncture holes in the can to make a round grater. Brilliant!

## Nuts

The most common nut in my cooking is the cashew. Have you ever seen the cashew fruit? People think that cashews grow just like other nuts, but in fact the cashew is a golden fruit and the little nut sits on the top. In this book I also use plenty of beautifully sweet pecans. Try them in my Pecan and Ginger Shortbread (*see* page 190), or Romesco Sauce (*see* page 36), which is my dub-it-up take on a gently spiced and nutty Spanish dish.

## Pineapple

On a trip to Jamaica I came across the Croydon Plantation, up in the hills above Montego Bay on the north coast, where I tasted six different kinds of pineapple. They tasted so different and each had its own texture. Pineapples grow from the ground, not down from a tree, and the sweetest part is nearest the soil. When you serve fresh pineapple, cut long wedges from top to bottom, so everyone gets a bit of the sweetest part. There are plenty of pineapple recipes in this book and I've even included one, Pine Drink (*see* page 26), that uses the peelings from the fruit.

## Pumpkin

'How does water walk to a pumpkin belly?' This is a childhood riddle. Here's the answer: the pumpkin can grow a long way from its root and the water travels along the stems. As kids, we used to trail the stem to see where it led. Pumpkin is a lovely juicy vegetable and I like the ones with deep reddish flesh. If you can't find a good pumpkin, use butternut squash instead. I like to put pumpkin in dishes such as rice and soups, so its flavours go right into the liquid, and it's also good sliced thinly and baked, such as in my Pumpkin and Spinach Gratin (*see* page 35).

## Rice

Rice with everything – well, at least a couple of times a week for me – and always on a Sunday in traditional Jamaican rice and peas! I love rice, the healthy brown variety as well as the white. Long-grain rice, such as basmati, is what I tend to use in my dishes. I sometimes like to add other ingredients to rice to make it more of a main event rather than a side dish, as in Roots' Rice (*see* page 128), Cuban Green Rice (*see* page 132) Red, Green and Gold Coconut Rice (*see* page 131) and Lazy Fish and Rice (*see* page 18).

## Rum

Lord-a-mercy! Rum is the beat behind the Caribbean party. In both food and drink recipes you can use clear rum or dark rum or – if you really want to put some buzz in your belly – get hold of the strong 'overproof' rum! Dark rum gets its colour from being aged in a wooden barrel, or because molasses is added, and has a deeper flavour. And rum is not just for cocktails; I've even got it in my Rum Tea Bread (*see* page 195)!

## Scotch bonnet chillies

I just couldn't live without the beautiful Bonnet! This is one of the most characteristic ingredients in Caribbean food. You can use other hot chillies but, for me, the Scotch Bonnet has such a beautiful fragrance and fruity flavour as well as heat. And they are hot, hot, hot! But each chilli varies, so try a little bit first to see. Leave out the seeds and the inner white ribs if you want to tame the flames. Scotch Bonnet chillies come in many different colours: they can be red, yellow, orange, green and even brown.

## Spring onions (scallions)

This is the main kind of onion I use, and I especially like the green tops for their vibrant colour and flavour. When you go to a market place in Jamaica, you often see a big bunch of juicy scallions tied together with a bunch of fragrant thyme because they are such good companions in the pot.

## Sugar

When I was growing up, we always had demerara sugar, which isn't as processed as white sugar so has more flavour. I also love muscovado sugar, both light and dark, as it has more of the tasty molasses than white sugar and adds a beautiful flavour to sweet and savoury dishes. Try the brown sugar icing on my Banana and Chocolate Chip Cake (*see* page 182) and the Muscovado Meringues (*see* page 159) to see what it's all about.

## Sweetcorn

Sweetcorn brings back happy memories of people coming round to see my childhood neighbour and relative, Mr Butler. They'd bring bags of corn and people would sit around preparing it for the pot. As we'd help out, everyone would tell stories…and massive lies! Then we had roast corn, boiled corn, corn porridge, crushed corn or cornmeal dumplings. If you want to try some different kinds of corn dishes, make my Crispy Corn Bread (*see* page 48) and the Cuban snack, fritoritos (*see* page 136).

## Sweet potatoes

I eat a lot of sweet potatoes. There's so much you can do with them – even make a traditional pudding flavoured with nutmeg and cinnamon (*see* page 174). You can buy white sweet potatoes, but the orange ones are more widely available. As well as putting them in soups and stews, or making them into a mash for the top of my Caribbean Spiced Shepherd's Pie (*see* page 95), they are great for roasting. Cut them into small pieces, coat them with olive oil and bung them in the oven, just as you would normal potatoes (we call those 'Irish potatoes' in the Caribbean).

## Thyme

Thyme is one of the most crucial flavourings in my food and another trusty member of my Sunshine Kit. Fish, meat, soups, baked dishes, marinades…thyme adds such fragrance to all of them. Often I just throw a whole sprig in – nice and easy – or sometimes strip the leaves off and use it like that. It's one of those ingredients that grows easily and so many people have it to hand. Food for free!

# Index

# Acknowledgements

My thanks are extended to: Hattie Ellis, Diana Henry, my son Zaion, Chris Terry, Karl Bridgeman, Sara Lewis, Becca Spry, Pene Parker, Leanne Bryan, Lucy Bannell, Natasha Eggough, Rodney Levine-Boateng, Miladis Diaz, Borra Garson and all the staff at DML.

Respect due to all my friends in my local Brixton Market especially Mr Porridge, Bridget Hugo and all the staff at Wild Caper.

Also my friends in Jamaica: Peter of Peter's Fish Stop in Discovery Bay, chef Christian Ghisays and all the staff at the Royal Plantation hotel, Ocho Rios and Tony Henry of Croydon Plantation.